OPPOSING
VIEWPOINTS®
SERIES

Stem Cells

Other Books of Related Interest:

Opposing Viewpoints Series
The Catholic Church

At Issue Series
Are Americans Overmedicated?
Human Embryo Experimentation

Current Controversies
The Elderly
Health Care
Medical Ethics

Global Viewpoints
Human Rights
Medical Ethics

Introducing Issues with Opposing Viewpoints
Vaccines

Issues That Concern You
Health Care

"Congress shall make no law . . . abridging the freedom of speech, or of the press."

First Amendment to the US Constitution

The basic foundation of our democracy is the First Amendment guarantee of freedom of expression. The Opposing Viewpoints Series is dedicated to the concept of this basic freedom and the idea that it is more important to practice it than to enshrine it.

Stem Cells

Jacqueline Langwith, Book Editor

GREENHAVEN PRESS
A part of Gale, Cengage Learning

GALE
CENGAGE Learning®

Detroit • New York • San Francisco • New Haven, Conn • Waterville, Maine • London

Elizabeth Des Chenes, *Managing Editor*

© 2012 Greenhaven Press, a part of Gale, Cengage Learning.

Gale and Greenhaven Press are registered trademarks used herein under license.

For more information, contact:
Greenhaven Press
27500 Drake Rd.
Farmington Hills, MI 48331-3535
Or you can visit our Internet site at gale.cengage.com

LIBRARY OF CONGRESS CATALOGING-IN-PUBLICATION DATA

Stem cells / Jacqueline Langwith, book editor.
p. cm. -- (Opposing viewpoints)
Includes bibliographical references and index.
ISBN 978-0-7377-5759-0 (hardcover) -- ISBN 978-0-7377-5760-6 (pbk.)
1. Stem cells--Public opinion. I. Langwith, Jacqueline.
QH588.S83S74295 2012
616'.0277--dc23
2011028271

Printed in Mexico
2 3 4 5 6 7 15 14 13 12

Contents

Chapter 3: What Kind of Embryos Should Be Used for Embryonic Stem Cell Research?

Chapter 4: What Role Should the Government Have in Stem Cell Research?

Why Consider Opposing Viewpoints?

> *"The only way in which a human being can make some approach to knowing the whole of a subject is by hearing what can be said about it by persons of every variety of opinion and studying all modes in which it can be looked at by every character of mind. No wise man ever acquired his wisdom in any mode but this."*
>
> John Stuart Mill

In our media-intensive culture it is not difficult to find differing opinions. Thousands of newspapers and magazines and dozens of radio and television talk shows resound with differing points of view. The difficulty lies in deciding which opinion to agree with and which "experts" seem the most credible. The more inundated we become with differing opinions and claims, the more essential it is to hone critical reading and thinking skills to evaluate these ideas. Opposing Viewpoints books address this problem directly by presenting stimulating debates that can be used to enhance and teach these skills. The varied opinions contained in each book examine many different aspects of a single issue. While examining these conveniently edited opposing views, readers can develop critical thinking skills such as the ability to compare and contrast authors' credibility, facts, argumentation styles, use of persuasive techniques, and other stylistic tools. In short, the Opposing Viewpoints Series is an ideal way to attain the higher-level thinking and reading skills so essential in a culture of diverse and contradictory opinions.

In addition to providing a tool for critical thinking, Opposing Viewpoints books challenge readers to question their own strongly held opinions and assumptions. Most people form their opinions on the basis of upbringing, peer pressure, and personal, cultural, or professional bias. By reading carefully balanced opposing views, readers must directly confront new ideas as well as the opinions of those with whom they disagree. This is not to simplistically argue that everyone who reads opposing views will—or should—change his or her opinion. Instead, the series enhances readers' understanding of their own views by encouraging confrontation with opposing ideas. Careful examination of others' views can lead to the readers' understanding of the logical inconsistencies in their own opinions, perspective on why they hold an opinion, and the consideration of the possibility that their opinion requires further evaluation.

Evaluating Other Opinions

To ensure that this type of examination occurs, Opposing Viewpoints books present all types of opinions. Prominent spokespeople on different sides of each issue as well as well-known professionals from many disciplines challenge the reader. An additional goal of the series is to provide a forum for other, less known, or even unpopular viewpoints. The opinion of an ordinary person who has had to make the decision to cut off life support from a terminally ill relative, for example, may be just as valuable and provide just as much insight as a medical ethicist's professional opinion. The editors have two additional purposes in including these less known views. One, the editors encourage readers to respect others' opinions—even when not enhanced by professional credibility. It is only by reading or listening to and objectively evaluating others' ideas that one can determine whether they are worthy of consideration. Two, the inclusion of such viewpoints encourages the important critical thinking skill of objectively evaluating an author's credentials and bias. This evaluation will illuminate an author's reasons for taking a particular stance on an issue and will aid in readers' evaluation of the author's ideas.

It is our hope that these books will give readers a deeper understanding of the issues debated and an appreciation of the complexity of even seemingly simple issues when good and honest people disagree. This awareness is particularly important in a democratic society such as ours in which people enter into public debate to determine the common good. Those with whom one disagrees should not be regarded as enemies but rather as people whose views deserve careful examination and may shed light on one's own.

Thomas Jefferson once said that "difference of opinion leads to inquiry, and inquiry to truth." Jefferson, a broadly educated man, argued that "if a nation expects to be ignorant and free . . . it expects what never was and never will be." As individuals and as a nation, it is imperative that we consider the opinions of others and examine them with skill and discernment. The Opposing Viewpoints Series is intended to help readers achieve this goal.

David L. Bender and Bruno Leone,
Founders

Introduction

"Fraudulent research is a particularly disturbing event, because it threatens an enterprise built on trust. Fortunately, such cases are rare—but they damage all of us."

Donald Kennedy,
editor in chief of the journal Science.

In March 2004 and June 2005, South Korean researcher Woo Suk Hwang made international headlines with the publication of two papers asserting that he and his colleagues at Seoul National University were the first scientists to successfully harvest human embryonic stem cells from cloned embryos. The South Korean government granted him the title of Supreme Scientist, stem cell researchers around the world hailed his scientific prowess, and many people were buoyed in their hopes for cures for debilitating diseases and injuries. Soon after the publication of Hwang's second paper, however, ethical questions about his research started emerging. Eventually, it was learned that some of Hwang's research procedures were unethical and that his results had been fabricated. He went from a being a national hero to an international disgrace. Hwang's apparent groundbreaking research and the subsequent scandal that followed drew a wide range of reactions from stem cell researchers and Americans supportive of and opposed to human embryonic stem cell research.

The Hwang saga began with the publications of two papers in *Science*, one of the most highly respected and widely read scientific journals in the world. In the March 2004 *Science* article, Hwang reported that he and his colleagues had produced a cloned human embryo and had then extracted embryonic stem cells from it. About a year later, in June 2005,

Hwang published another paper in *Science*, claiming that he had optimized the cloning procedure and was able to produce not just one, but eleven human embryos and was able to create stem cell lines from them. Furthermore, according to Hwang, the eleven stem cell lines were genetically matched to patients suffering from diabetes and other diseases. Because patient-specific stem cells should not trigger the body's immune system mechanisms, their generation is considered a significant milestone in bringing stem cell treatments closer to reality. In the spring of 2004 and the summer of 2005, newspapers, the Internet, and television programs around the world were filled with stories noting the importance of Hwang's research accomplishments. In a May 20, 2005, article in the journal *Nature*, another of the world's premier scientific journals, Harvard University stem cell scientist George Daley called Hwang's research "spectacular" and said "it's moved the field so far forward and so much more quickly than anticipated."

Some American supporters of embryonic stem cell research found it frustrating that such a significant research accomplishment occurred outside the United States. They felt that it illustrated how stem cell research in the United States was lagging behind that in other countries because of government restrictions on federal funding. In 2001, President George W. Bush had limited federal funding to research using only stem cell lines already in existence. Embryonic stem cell research proponents, such as political journalist and author Michael Kinsley, believed these restrictions were impeding American research, and Hwang's achievements as reported in *Science* seemed to back this up. In a May 20, 2005, essay published in the *Minneapolis Star Tribune*, Kinsley wrote, "Imagine what it's like to open the newspaper (as I did Friday morning) and read that scientists in South Korea have made a huge breakthrough toward curing a disease that is slowly wrecking your life. But your own government is trying to prevent that cure." Kinsley suffers from Parkinson's disease, which is one of the many diseases that embryonic stem cell researchers hope to cure.

While Kinsley was frustrated with the news coming from South Korea, people who believe human embryonic stem cell research is morally wrong were troubled by it. Richard Doerflinger, the associate director of the Secretariat of Pro-Life Activities of the US Conference of Catholic Bishops (USCCB), maintains that human embryonic stem research is immoral because it is based on the destruction of a human embryo. The USCCB also contends that therapeutic cloning, or the production of cloned human embryos for research purposes, is morally wrong. Doerflinger's response to Hwang's apparent stem cell breakthrough was noted in a May 20, 2005, *New York Times* article by science writer Gina Kolata in which he was quoted to have said: "Up until now, people were beginning to wonder whether human cloning for any purpose was feasible at all. This development makes it feasible enough to be a clear and present danger." Kolata also captured the reaction of Leon Kass, a medical expert and chairman of President Bush's Council on Bioethics. According to Kass, "Whatever its technical merit, this research is morally troubling: it creates human embryos solely for research, makes it much easier to produce cloned babies, and exploits women as egg donors not for their benefits."

By the end of 2005, Doerflinger, Daley, and many other people would be commenting not on the merits or immorality of Hwang's research, but on its deception. It appeared that Hwang had acted unethically to obtain the human egg cells he needed to conduct the cloning procedure. Hwang had resorted to paying some women for the egg cells and had pressured female researchers in his lab to donate their egg cells. While these claims were being investigated it was found that Hwang had not done what he had said he had. In January of 2006, Seoul National University (SNU) issued a report stating that Hwang's laboratory "does not possess patient-specific stem cell lines or any scientific basis for claiming to have created one." On January 16, 2006, the editors of *Science* retracted both of Hwang's papers, writing, "Because the final report of the SNU investigation indicated that a significant amount of the data presented in both papers is fabricated, the editors of *Science* feel that an immediate and unconditional retraction of both papers is needed. We therefore retract these two papers and advise the scientific community that the results reported in them are deemed to be invalid." On the day the conclusions of the SNU investigation were released, *Washington Post* science writers Anthony Faiola and Rick Weiss wrote, "The deception means that the highly touted field of embryonic stem cell research is years behind where scientists thought it was."

The scientific community immediately began looking within and wondering how the scandal could have occurred. Scientists from around the world questioned how a publication of the stature of *Science* could have published fraudulent research. The journal began reviewing its procedures for accepting and publishing papers in an effort to understand and prevent such a scandal from happening again.

While the scientific community scrambled to reassure the public that scientists could still be trusted, those who opposed human embryonic stem cell research determined that the scandal was a reflection of the entire field of stem cell research. While testifying in front of a US congressional committee in March 2006, the USCCB's Doerflinger stated, "It is generally true that a discovery of fraud in one researcher's claims does not discredit an entire field. But in this case, Dr. Hwang's studies *were* the field of allegedly successful human cloning for research purposes. If his research is a fraud, there is (at present) nothing left of that field." In his testimony, Doerflinger also asserted that misrepresenting the truth and creating and destroying embryos for research purposes go hand in hand. Said Doerflinger, "Cloning advocates have brushed aside moral concerns about human life, and the indignity of creating new lives just to destroy them. In any case, we should not be surprised when an ethic that dismisses 'Thou shalt not kill' in the quest for cures applies the same calculus to 'Thou shalt not bear false witness.' If the embryo's 'merely biological' life can be trampled to benefit more valuable lives, 'merely factual' truth can be sacrificed for the higher truth of progress."

Despite Doerflinger's statement, most stem cell scientists felt that the scandal was not a reflection on the entire stem cell field. They believed that although the scandal damaged the field of stem cell research, the damage was not irreparable. In a February 3, 2006, article in the *Chronicle of Higher Education*, George Daley, who originally had thought Hwang's research was "spectacular," tried to put the scandal in perspective. "I don't know how anybody could argue that it's a step backward," said Daley. "It's simply that a breakthrough that folks had believed has been made hasn't been made." When Daley's Harvard University colleague Doug Melton was asked by Claudia Dreifus of the *New York Times* whether the scandal made his work harder, he replied, "It has to raise, in the public's mind, the question as to whether there's legitimacy to this kind of science. Fortunately, stem cell research is not dependent on one discovery. Even though Hwang's findings turned out to be fraudulent, nothing he claimed was a fundamental challenge to the principles of embryonic stem cell research."

Since the scandal has occurred, the field of stem cell science has generally moved on and made advances that might please Daley, Kinsley, *and* Doerflinger. In 2007, researchers produced human pluripotent stem cells from an adult skin cell. These "induced pluripotent stem cells," or iPSCs, may have the same therapeutic potential as human embryonic stem cells without the destruction of embryos. When they were first produced, many people touted the production of iP-SCs as an advance that may end many of the moral debates about stem cell research.

In *Opposing Viewpoints: Stem Cells*, the authors explore the issues surrounding stem cell research in viewpoints addressing the following chapter-heading questions: What Is the Therapeutic Potential of Stem Cell Treatments? Is Stem Cell Research Moral? What Kind of Embryos Should Be Used for Embryonic Stem Cell Research? and What Role Should the Government Have in Stem Cell Research? As is shown by the many conflicting opinions expressed herein, it is clear that the debate about stem cell research rages on.

What Is the Therapeutic Potential of Stem Cell Treatments?

Chapter Preface

"It was meant to be," twenty-one-year-old Timothy J. Atchison from Alabama told the *Washington Post*'s Rob Stein regarding being the first patient to receive a human embryonic stem cell treatment authorized by the US Food and Drug Administration (FDA). On September 25, 2010, Atchison, known as T.J. to his friends, was involved in a serious car accident that left him paralyzed from the chest down. Around the same time, researchers from the California biotechnology company Geron were looking to enroll the first patient in the first-ever clinical trial for an embryonic stem cell treatment. The patient needed to be an adult who had suffered a recent injury to the thoracic portion of the spinal cord, which left him or her completely paralyzed from the waist down. Meant to be or not, Atchison fit the bill, and seven days after his accident he was injected with embryonic stem cells.

Ever since they were first produced by James Thomson in 1998, human embryonic stem cells have been a source of hope for people with debilitating injuries or disease. Since then, scientists at universities and biotechnology companies around the United States and throughout the world have been trying to develop practical treatments that turn the promise of embryonic stem cells into reality.

Before an embryonic stem cell treatment can be offered to the American public, it must be approved by the FDA. The FDA considers stem cells to be "new drugs" and requires them to go through the same type of approval process as other new drugs. This process involves at least two clinical trials where the new drug is tested on humans and its safety and effectiveness are monitored. The FDA only allows new drugs to proceed to a clinical trial when laboratory and animal tests indicate that the drug is likely to be safe and work well in humans.

Geron was the first company to receive FDA approval to test an embryonic stem cell treatment on humans. For many years the company, which funded Thomson's pioneering 1998 research, has worked to develop embryonic stem cell treatments for diseases such as diabetes and heart disease. It was the company's embryonic stem cell treatment for spinal cord injuries, called GRNOPC1, however, that most quickly proceeded through the development process. GRNOPC1 is composed of nerve cells called oligodendrocytes that were created from embryonic stem cells obtained from days-old embryos leftover from fertility treatments. People with spinal cord injuries suffer a loss of oligodendrocytes, which generally leads to paralysis. According to Geron, studies using animal models showed that GRNOPC1 could restore movement in paralyzed animals, and would be safe and effective for people.

After submitting an application containing more than twenty thousand pages of data and waiting nearly a year, in January 2009 Geron received approval from the FDA to test GRNOPC1 on humans. In a company press release Thomas Okarma, Geron's president, spoke about the significance of the FDA's clearance to proceed, saying, "This marks the beginning of what is potentially a new chapter in medical therapeutics—one that reaches beyond pills to a new level of healing: the restoration of organ and tissue function achieved by the injection of healthy replacement cells." The GRNOPC1 human trials did not happen right away. They were put on hold for more than a year, while Geron addressed concerns that the cells could cause cancerous tumors. In July 2010, after Geron assured the FDA that the treatment was safe, the FDA finally lifted the hold. Responding to the news, Geron's Okarma said, "We jumped through a lot of hoops to convince a lot of audiences. No one wants another Jesse Gelsinger." Okarma was referring to a tragic event that had occurred more than a decade earlier. In 1999, Jesse Gelsinger volunteered to participate in a clinical study looking into the safety and effectiveness of another potentially miraculous medical treatment—gene therapy. Tragically, Gelsinger died as a result of the experimental treatment and the field of gene therapy never recovered.

Geron began readying itself for the trials. The company spent months training special teams of doctors at seven secret sites around the country to be ready to act quickly as soon as a suitable patient was identified. The teams then had to wait for a patient who met the study's enrollment criteria; that is, an adult who had been completely paralyzed from the chest down within the previous two weeks. On a late September night, T.J. Atchison became the first patient to meet the study's requirements.

A few days after his accident, Atchison was sent to the Shepard Center, a spinal cord and brain injury rehabilitation facility in Atlanta, Georgia, and one of the seven sites with teams ready to administer GRNOPC1. When doctors asked him whether he would consider being the first person to have an experimental drug made from human embryonic stem cells injected into his body, Atchison said yes. Nearly six months later he told the *Washington Post*'s Rob Stein that as he was being tested to make sure he met the study's criteria and would be eligible to have his back cut open and have two million oligodendrocyte cells infused into his spine, he turned to one of the doctors and told her that if he passed all the tests, "then it's God's will."

It is likely that the name T.J. Atchison will forever be associated with embryonic stem cell research. It will take time before scientists are able to determine whether the treatment helped him; however, his progress, and that of other recipients of experimental embryonic stem cell treatments, will probably be the source of debates about the effectiveness of such treatments for years to come. In the following chapter, patients, scientists, and others provide differing opinions on the therapeutic potential of stem cell treatments.

"[Stem cell] research is real, promising, and hopeful to me and to others as we want so much to . . . win our battles over diseases that constantly challenge our quality of life."

Embryonic Stem Cells Can Cure Diseases

Cody Unser

Cody Unser is the oldest daughter of champion racecar driver Al Unser Jr. and granddaughter of four-time Indianapolis 500 winner Al Unser Sr. At the age of twelve, Cody was paralyzed from the waist down after contracting transverse myelitis, a rare autoimmune disease. In the following viewpoint, Cody testifies before a US congressional committee about the hope that human embryonic stem cell research offers her and millions of other Americans suffering with debilitating injuries and diseases. According to Unser, hope became a part of her life the day she saw the recovery of a once-paralyzed mouse treated with embryonic stem cells. Unser urges the committee members to help her beat her disease by passing legislation that explicitly allows embryonic stem cell research to proceed in the United States.

As you read, consider the following questions:

1. Transverse myelitis is an autoimmune disease that causes the immune system to attack what, according to Unser?

2. What does the author say a once-paralyzed mouse that was treated with embryonic stem cells was able to do?

3. According to Unser, if Congress and the courts keep debating human embryonic stem cell research, more and more scientists will have no choice but to do what?

Thank you Chairman Harkin for allowing me to testify and use my voice on behalf of millions of Americans living with debilitating diseases. I feel very honored and, to be honest, frustrated as to why we are here today.

Ten years ago, my hero, my superman, Christopher Reeve, sat in his power wheelchair and using every breath he took thanks to a machine, testified to Congress with the hope that embryonic stem cell research would be federally funded. Today, in 2010, we are still fighting for this promising and hopeful research to continue. Embryonic stem cells are science based on hope. Hope for improving the quality of life of millions of Americans by providing better treatment and eventually cures.

Living with Paralysis and Disease

My journey began 11 years ago. I was a healthy 12-year-old kid who was very active and had big dreams. Everything changed on February 5, 1999. I can't recall how it felt to put my feet on the floor, how I got dressed that morning or what I had for breakfast but what I do remember is that in a manner of 20 minutes my body became paralyzed and my life drastically changed. I was playing basketball at school and suddenly couldn't catch my breath and my head started pounding with sharp pain. The school I was attending called the ambulance and while laying down in the locker room my left leg became numb and tingly. I picked it up, put it back down and I couldn't feel the floor. I was scared out of my mind but I thought that whatever was wrong the doctors could fix. Transverse Myelitis is an autoimmune disorder in which the immune system attacks the spinal cord causing inflammation that damages the cells that control sensory [input] and movement of the body. After staying in the hospital for a couple of months I went to rehabilitation where I learned how to do everything from a wheelchair all the while having dreams of my feet imprinting in the sand.

Today I am a 23-year-old woman who has learned to adapt to life in a wheelchair and in a paralyzed body. Even though I live life to the fullest and look as though I am just sitting down in a wheelchair, I have to always worry about pressure sores from constant sitting, I worry about my osteoporosis advancing in my bones from not standing and bearing weight which led to a fracture of my left femur. I worry about my scoliosis getting worse, a curvature of the spine common in people with spinal cord injuries. I have bladder and bowel complications and advancing nerve pain. But I am just one out of millions of Americans living with various diseases and conditions that no matter how hard we try affect how we live our lives.

Embryonic Stem Cells Give Hope

The first time hope actually meant something to me and became sort of my religion was when I saw what human embryonic stem cells can do. A year after I became paralyzed, my doctor and stem cell scientist, Doug Kerr, who was at Johns Hopkins [University] at the time, showed me a mouse that was once paralyzed and now can bear its weight and take steps. At that moment, I realized that this is science I couldn't ignore and it gave me a feeling of hope I wanted to fight for. Which brings me to another point. It's frustrating to hear critics of this research say this is a path we can't go down and

The Promise of Stem Cells

Studying stem cells will help us understand how they transform into the dazzling array of specialized cells that make us what we are. Some of the most serious medical conditions, such as cancer and birth defects, are due to problems that occur somewhere in this process. A better understanding of normal cell development will allow us to understand and perhaps correct the errors that cause these medical conditions.

Another potential application of stem cells is making cells and tissues for medical therapies. Today, donated organs and tissues are often used to replace those that are diseased or destroyed. Unfortunately, the number of people needing a transplant far exceeds the number of organs available for transplantation. Pluripotent stem cells offer the possibility of a renewable source of replacement cells and tissues to treat a myriad of diseases, conditions, and disabilities, including Parkinson's disease, amyotrophic lateral sclerosis, spinal cord injury, burns, heart disease, diabetes, and arthritis.

National Institutes of Health,
Stem Cell Information, 2011.

adult stem cells hold just as much promise as embryonic stem cells do. Science is the pursuit of discovery and possibility. We should explore every opportunity and not count anything out because I can't wait. And I know millions of Americans now and in the future can't wait. In Christopher Reeve's testimony in 2000 he said, "No obstacle should stand in the way of responsible investigation of these possibilities." I am here today to remove yet another obstacle in the path of this research, this answer, this hope.

The political debate over this research is forcing many of our brilliant scientists to think twice about whether they should stay in this field. I know how dedicated and passionate they are about helping all of us find answers to our pain and suffering. If we keep dragging this debate back here to Washington, in Congress and in the courts, more and more scientists will have no choice but to either find a different research avenue or move to another country where they can pursue the promise that embryonic stem cells possess. Once and for all I urge Congress to pass unambiguous legislation that allows this research to move forward.

I grew up around racetracks and my family has won the Indianapolis 500 a total of 9 times. The goal of every driver is to pass under the black-and-white checkered flag first. The meaning of the checkered flag is winning. Right now, I can see that flag waving for me to go by. But with this current [August 23, 2010,] court ruling [blocking federal funding of human embryonic stem cell research] I feel that I have been driving under a long yellow caution flag. Today, I came here to say that this research is real, promising, and hopeful to me and to others as we want so much to take that checkered flag and win our battles over diseases that constantly challenge our quality of life.

| *"If [embryonic stem cell] cures are just around the corner, this corner is far, far away."*

Embryonic Stem Cell Cures Are Still Years Away

Michael Fumento

Michael Fumento is an attorney, author, and investigative reporter. His articles appear frequently in Forbes, Reason, *the* Washington Times, *and the* Rocky Mountain News. *In the following viewpoint, Fumento asserts that the timeline for human embryonic stem cell (ESC) cures is still far in the future. According to Fumento, it will be twenty, thirty, or even fifty years or more before ESC research fulfills any of its promises—if it ever does. He argues that the federal government should stop funding ESC research and direct its money to other, more ethical and more successful research, such as adult stem cell research or induced pluripotent stem cell research.*

As you read, consider the following questions:

1. At which university and in whose laboratory does the author say the first human embryonic stem cell culture was created?

2. According to Fumento, what does James Thomson say is to blame for the long time frame for embryonic stem cell research cures?

3. According to the author, how many clinical trials have adult stem cells been used in?

An age of medical miracles is dawning. [Barack] Obama administration federal funding rules for embryonic stem cells, or ES cells, will open wide the money floodgates for "the most remarkable potential of any scientific discovery ever made with respect to human health." It has "the capacity to cure maladies of all sorts, including cancer, heart disease, Parkinson's, Alzheimer's," and spinal cord injuries. Or so says Sen. Arlen Specter (D-Pa.) among others.

Cures Are Decades Away

But quadriplegics probably shouldn't sign up for the New York City Marathon just yet. If these cures are just around the corner, this corner is far, far away. And that's according to ES cell researchers and funding advocates themselves. The time frame for the first of those miracles seems routinely to be given as a "decade," as in "a decade away" or "a decade off." And it keeps shifting.

Thus it appeared in a 1998 newswire article heralding the creation of the first human ES cell culture in James Thomson's University of Wisconsin lab. Thomson and his fellow researchers "warn that such clinical applications are perhaps as much as a decade away," said the article. Perhaps as much? Check your calendar. Addressing a 2007 Wisconsin convention nine years later, Thomson articulated that the time frame had shifted to "decades away," plural.

The scientist didn't blame too little federal funding, as have others, according to the Associated Press [AP]. . . . Rather Thomson blamed simple biology. Among other problems, ES cells require permanent use of dangerous immunosuppressive

Law of Exaggerated Expectations

Five and even ten years have come and gone, and there are no treatments or cures using hESCs [human embryonic stem cells]. One clinical trial approved by the FDA [Food and Drug Administration] in 2009, then put on safety hold, was reapproved in July 2010, but as yet, not a single patient has even been injected with hESC. The five- to ten-year predictions were apparently designed to mislead people into thinking treatments were imminent, and to realize them, all Congress needed to do was expand federal hESCR funding.

In 1992, journalist Gregg Easterbrook, writing on the global warming debate, coined what he called the "Law of Doomsaying": "Predict dreadful events whose arrival impends no sooner than 5 years hence, no later than 10"—i.e., soon enough to scare people into action, but far enough away that they will not recall if your predictions prove wrong. In the hESCR debate, let's call it the "Law of Exaggerated Expectations": Predict wildly optimistic outcomes for cures no later than ten years hence, but no sooner than five years away—a seemingly reasonable time to raise expectations and support for the research, but far enough off that people will forget if it is wrong.

Gene Tarne and David Prentice,
American Thinker, *August 8, 2010.*

drugs. They have a nasty tendency to form tumors both malignant and benign including teratomas—meaning "monster tumor." Teratomas can grow larger than a football and can contain eyeball parts, hair, and teeth. Yech!

Okay, so how many "decades?"

"The routine utilization of human embryonic stem cells for medicine is 20 to 30 years hence," embryonic stem cell research advocate William Haseltine and then–chief executive officer of Human Genome Sciences told Agence France Presse in 2001. "The timeline to commercialization is so long that I simply would not invest," he added.

Some ES cell researchers believe "three to five decades" is a realistic timeline, while British fertility expert Lord Robert Winston said in a 2005 lecture, "I am not entirely convinced that embryonic stem cells will, in my lifetime, and possibly anybody's lifetime for that matter, be holding quite the promise that we desperately hope they will."

The Imperial College, London University professor insisted research "should be conducted, and I believe is totally ethical." But, he added, "One of the problems is that in order to persuade the public that we must do this work, we often go rather too far in promising what we might achieve. . . . "

One wonders if ES cell research patient-advocates like Michael J. Fox, Michael Kinsley, and Mary Tyler Moore would be so enthusiastic if they knew this.

ES Cells Are Obsolete

That's especially so given that ES cells are hardly the end-all and be-all of regenerative medicine, with stiff competition from adult stem cells (AS cells) and what are called "induced pluripotent stem cells." These iPS cells, engineered from mature human skin cells, are just as flexible as embryonic ones. But as with the AS variety, they have neither the health concerns nor moral baggage of the embryonic ones.

Tellingly, the AP article about Thomson's 2007 speech said, "One day, some believe [ES] cells will become sources of brain tissue, muscle and bone marrow to replace diseased or injured body parts." Which is to say they may be able to do what AS cells have already been doing for years, either routinely or experimentally. Life-saving marrow regeneration with stem cells dates back to 1956.

AS cells have now treated scores of illnesses, including many cancers, autoimmune disease, cardiovascular disease, immunodeficiency disorders, neural degenerative diseases, anemias and other blood conditions. They've been used in over 2,000 human clinical trials. There has never been an ES cell clinical trial. Former National Institutes of Health director Dr. Bernadine Healy, once an ES cell research "enthusiast," now calls them "obsolete."

That's why it hardly makes sense to vastly increase federal research funding for ES cells. Medical research spending is always a zero sum game. However big the overall budget, every dollar approved for one grant is a dollar lost to others.

In justifying his stem cell research executive order, President Barack Obama cited "a consensus" of "the majority of Americans." Actually, the polling responses vary tremendously depending on the questions asked. But no decision is better than the information upon which it's based. What might Americans think if they knew the ES cell research "decades away" secret?

> "Adult stem cells aren't just showing great promise but are treating people now."

Adult Stem Cells Are Already Curing Diseases

Jean Peduzzi Nelson

On September 16, 2010, a US congressional committee held a hearing on the promise of stem cell research. Jean Peduzzi Nelson, a stem cell researcher from Wayne State University in Detroit, Michigan, was one of the scientists invited to testify. In the following excerpt from her testimony, Nelson says that even though adult stem cell research receives very little funding, these types of stem cells are showing more than promise, they are helping people now. According to Nelson, adult stem cells are already being used to help people with a wide range of maladies, such as heart disease, spinal cord injury, corneal blindness, and sickle-cell anemia. She urges the US government to direct more funding to adult stem cell research so that more people can be helped.

As you read, consider the following questions:

1. What does Nelson say is the financial challenge associated with adult stem cells?

2. What does an American spinal injury Grade A indicate, according to the author?

3. What disease does Barry Goudy, as mentioned by Nelson, suffer from, and in what year did he receive adult stem cell treatment?

There are two major categories of stem cells: embryonic and adult. Human embryonic stem cells are derived from human embryos and remain controversial. I want to focus my comments on the science of adult stem cells that are treating patients for many diseases. This second category of stem cells can be obtained from adult tissues, as well as tissues from children. For my purposes, I will use "adult stem cells" to refer to these as well as stem cells from umbilical cord blood. . . .

Adult Stem Cells Are Best

Stem cells are cells that can generate lots of cells and, under the right conditions, become one of the many cell types in the body. Adult stem cells are stem cells obtained from adults, children, even infants and umbilical cord after birth. These include cells from the bone marrow, nose, fat tissue, umbilical cord and other places. The great thing about these cells is that a person's own cells can be used, which eliminates the problem of immune rejection and tumor formation sometimes observed with other types of stem cells. Adult stem cells are the best stem cells to replace lost or damaged cells in our bodies.

The financial challenge with adult stem cells is that when you use your own cells, there is usually no intellectual property or patents [involved]. So, the biotech industry that invests *billions* in research often does not fund this research. Millions of dollars are needed to complete each clinical trial so all pa-

Adult Stem Cells in Human Testing

For all the emotional debate that began about a decade ago on allowing the use of embryonic stem cells, it's adult stem cells that are in human testing today. An extensive review of stem cell projects and interviews with two dozen experts reveal a wide range of potential treatments.

Adult stem cells are being studied in people who suffer from multiple sclerosis, heart attacks and diabetes. Some early results suggest stem cells can help some patients avoid leg amputation. Recently, researchers reported that they restored vision to patients whose eyes were damaged by chemicals.

Apart from these efforts, transplants of adult stem cells have become a standard lifesaving therapy for perhaps hundreds of thousands of people with leukemia, lymphoma and other blood diseases.

"That's really one of the great success stories of stem cell biology that gives us all hope," says Dr. David Scadden of Harvard, who notes stem cells are also used to grow skin grafts.

Malcolm Ritter,
USA Today, *August 4, 2010.*

tients can benefit from a treatment, not the lucky few, and so that billions can be saved in health care costs. NIH [National Institutes of Health] has developed new programs to encourage translational research and clinical trials, but has a much smaller budget than private industry. Much of the funding for adult stem cells by NIH is directed at older but important uses of bone marrow stem cells that were developed in the '50s and '60s for leukemia and other cancers. While bone marrow transplants have been used in patients for years, the successful isolation and characterization of adult stem cells is a very recent science. The first mouse adult stem cell was successfully isolated and purified in the laboratory in 1988. The first human adult stem cell was first successfully isolated and characterized in the laboratory in 1992. New uses of adult stem cells for other diseases and injuries only started in the '90s, but have already reached patients with various diseases and injuries as I will demonstrate.

Patients Who Have Been Helped

I would like to tell you about 5 patients who have been helped by adult stem cells. These patients were either part of a clinical trial, and their results are now published in a peer-reviewed journal, or sometimes a similar procedure was done in a clinical trial that is now published.

The first patient is Silvio, whom I met several years ago. I have been working with a group in Portugal led by Dr. Carlos Lima. Dr. Lima, Dr. Pratas-Vital, Dr. Escada, Dr. Capucho, and Dr. Hasse-Ferreira have been using a person's own tissue from inside of the nose as a way of delivering adult stem cells. Silvio had a spinal cord injury at the base of his neck [which is classified as a Grade A injury, according to the] . . . American Spinal Injury Association Impairment Scale (AIS). . . . Grade A is considered the worst, which indicates a "complete" spinal cord injury where no motor or sensory function is preserved in the sacral segments S4–S5. Silvio was left with no movement of his legs and minimal movement of his fingers. At 2 years after injury, he received his own adult stem cells and partial scar removal after intensive rehab failed to lead to an improvement.

Today he can maintain standing position and wave without help. With a walker and short braces, he can walk over 30 feet without anyone helping him. He can now move his fingers, which he could not do before. . . .

Silvio is not an isolated case. Here are the 2 peer-reviewed publications from the *Journal of Spinal Cord Medicine* and *Neurorehabilitation and Neural Repair* which reveal that more than half of AIS A patients improved in grade compared to the normal 5% [that improve] without treatment. When the adult stem cells are combined with an effective rehab program, 12/13 [twelve of thirteen] AIS A [patients] improved in AIS grade and all of the patients regained some muscle movement in their legs. . . .

The next [patient] is Doug Rice, who was told in 1998 that he had 2 years to live due to chronic heart failure after multiple heart attacks. At that time he could hardly walk. He did not qualify for any US clinical trials, so he went to Thailand to have a treatment with adult stem cells. The cells were sent to a company in Israel where the cells were purified and allowed to multiply, then sent back to Thailand for injection. Since that time, he has more energy and is enjoying life. However, this is also not an isolated incident. This year [2010,] an article was published in the *European Journal of Heart Failure* reporting the follow-up of 191 patients who received adult stem cells from their own bone marrow compared to 200 patients with comparable symptoms. These adult stem cell–treated patients lived longer and had a greater capacity to do exercises. Their heart functioned much better based on a large number of tests (left ventricular ejection fraction, cardiac index, oxygen uptake, and left ventricle contractility). This report of the STAR-heart study [of the clinical use of adult stem cells for treating heart disease] provides the controlled clinical trial data, and new trials are now proceeding in the US. . . .

More Cures

Corneal disease is the 2nd leading cause of blindness after cataracts in the world. Corneal transplants are commonly used, but the transplants are rejected in about 20% of the cases. . . . [Three] patients [who had severe burns or damage to their eyes and suffered from corneal blindness] had surgery on their eyes, but these surgeries did not help. Several years later, adult stem cells were removed from the opposite eye and implanted in the damaged eye. . . . The patients went from barely being able to see hand movements to normal sight in these eyes. This procedure was successful in more than 75% of the 112 patients. Some of these patients were followed for 10 years. We need more clinical studies in the US to treat US patients with corneal blindness.

The next patient is Joe Davis Jr. Joe . . . was born with severe sickle cell anemia. Sickle cell anemia is a blood disease that affects 1/500 [one out of five hundred] African-Americans. The doctors thought that Joe might not live to see his teens. When Joe was 2 years old in 2002, he received a transplant of stem cells from his younger brother's umbilical cord. Joe no longer has sickle cell anemia. So, where are we now? About 72,000 people in the US have sickle cell anemia that causes pain, chronic tiredness from anemia and severe infections, usually beginning when they are babies. In a published study last year [2009] in the *New England Journal of Medicine* that was supported by NIH, ten adults were treated with adult stem cells from their brother or sister. Of these patients, nine no longer had symptoms of sickle cell anemia and were doing well at 4 years after their treatment. A similar study was published in 2008 showing that 6/7 of the children with severe sickle cell anemia treated in a similar manner were without sickle cell symptoms when they were examined at 2–8 years after treatment. It would be great if we could have everyone with sickle cell anemia treated.

The last [patient] is Barry Goudy, who was suffering from multiple sclerosis [MS]. He had numerous relapses and the medication was not helping his condition. He was part of a study conducted at Northwestern Memorial Hospital in Chicago and received his own stem cells in 2003. His MS symptoms disappeared in 4 months, and he continues to be symptom free today. Results were published last year by Burt and colleagues in *Lancet*. Patients had what is known as relapsing-remitting MS. These were patients who were still having relapses despite interferon beta treatment. All of the treated patients did not show the normal progressive worsening associated with MS, and a significant functional improvement was noted in these patients. In a similar study published this year, they describe the one-year follow-up of 6 patients who showed improvement when their muscles were evaluated using electrophysiology. Their condition either stayed the same or improved in a disease that is characterized with progressive decline in function.

Progress, Not Just Promise

[These patients] and their related clinical trials using adult stem cells show amazing progress for severe spinal cord injury, chronic heart failure, corneal blindness, sickle cell anemia, and multiple sclerosis. However, this is not an exhaustive list of the recent clinical trial findings using adult stem cells. I would just like to mention the amazing progress using adult stem cells in juvenile diabetes. A recent clinical trial report in the *Journal of the American Medical Association* found that the majority of the 23 patients who received adult stem cells achieved insulin independence in the 2-year follow-up. Many [of you] may remember the news report of the person who received a new trachea using adult stem cells. An article published this year details the recovery of 20 patients with upper airway problems that received adult stem cells. Another breakthrough article was published this year in [the journal] *Blood* which calls the use of adult stem cells ". . . the gold standard in the frontline therapy of younger patients with multiple myeloma because it results in higher complete remission and longer event-free survival than conventional chemotherapy.

Only with the help of NIH and the DOD [Department of Defense] Congressionally Directed Medical Research Programs can these successful treatments reach all the people that desperately need them. . . . These pioneers need to be joined by many other people to help those suffering from diseases and injuries. Adult stem cells aren't just showing great promise but are treating people now. Much more of the limited funding needs to be directed at adult stem cells that are showing success right now.

| "Questionable stem-cell therapies have led to the death and hospitalisation of a number of patients this year."

People Should Be Wary of Overseas Stem Cell Clinics Offering Cures

Michael Brooks

Michael Brooks is a writer for the New Statesman, *a British current affairs and politics magazine. In the following viewpoint, Brooks asserts that patients must be suspicious of new stem cell therapies now available at clinics around the world. Although Brooks acknowledges that stem cell research holds enormous potential, he cautions that stem cell treatments are still in their infancy, and that there are also some unscrupulous scientists profiting from hopeful patients. Many stem cell clinics, says Brooks, offer unproven and risky treatments, so prospective patients need to beware. Until there is both a global agreement on stem cell research, along with regulations in place, Brooks believes the unsafe practices that come along with stem cell tourism will continue.*

As you read, consider the following questions:

1. What are some of the diseases, listed by Brooks, that scientists hope to cure with stem cell therapy?

2. Why, according to Brooks, is stem cell tourism "necessary"?

3. Why is stem cell therapy only illegal in China "in theory," according to the author?

Stem-cell therapy is about to prove itself. Over the next few months, researchers will inject stem cells into the retinas of 12 people with a genetic condition that has slowly robbed them of their eyesight. The hope — and expectation — is that these people will begin to see again in 2011.

Great Potential

The cells, derived from human embryos, have the ability to develop into virtually any kind of cell in the body. The patients in the trial have faulty retinal cells that began to die off in early childhood. These cells are meant to supply nutrients to the photoreceptor cells that capture light; when they fail, the result is gradually degenerating vision. In many cases, the sufferers can do little more than see their hands in front of their face or perceive a difference between light and shade. An injection of 200,000 embryonic stem cells should reverse this because they will develop into healthy versions of the defective ones and restore the support system for photoreceptors.

A Closer Look

Crucially for the reputation of stem-cell scientists, the trial can be halted at any stage. Because of their position on the retina, the cells can be seen with a microscope and removed, should anything untoward start to occur.

Scientists hope that the extreme versatility of embryonic stem cells will eventually help people suffering from a wide range of medical problems, from heart disease to Parkinson's. Yet there are also some unscrupulous scientists playing on— and profiting from—this hope.

Questionable stem-cell therapies have led to the death and hospitalisation of a number of patients this year. Among the deaths were two Koreans who indulged in "stem-cell tourism": their cells were prepared in Seoul but administered in China and Japan.

Stem Cell Tourism

Such tourism is necessary because performing stem-cell therapy is illegal in South Korea, though perhaps not for long. The Korea Times reported last month that lawmakers, officials and entertainers were being offered illegal stem-cell treatments at reduced cost in exchange for help relaxing the Korean regulations.

In theory, administering stem-cell therapy is also illegal in China, but regulatory guidelines have yet to be drafted, so there is a window of opportunity for physicians willing to offer the treatment. In Japan, approval is required to perform stem-cell therapies but physicians are allowed to import stem cells for use in private practice. Until there is global agreement and enforcement of regulations, stem-cell tourism will continue.

The Future of Stem Cell Therapy

The inevitable deaths and disappointments are likely to taint the reputation of stem-cell therapy for some time.

The science is still at its earliest stages, but this kind of therapy could offer us what looks like a series of miracle cures. It would be a disaster if proper trials or public acceptance were stymied because of profiteering.

> "Patients in need will seek out untested
> technologies as soon as the promised
> benefits outweigh the perceived risks."

Desperation Forces Sick People to Risk Overseas Stem Cell Treatment

Aaron Saenz

Aaron Saenz is a physicist and a senior editor at Singularity Hub, *a blog and news network covering stem cells, robots, genetics, artificial intelligence, and other futuristic topics. In the following viewpoint, Saenz contends that international stem cell clinics will continue to draw patients because the treatments provide hope to those in need of cures. Saenz maintains that the bureaucratic and political obstacles that stem cell treatments face in the United States will push many people to travel to clinics around the world. According to Saenz, patients suffering from conditions that could be helped by stem cell treatments will accept the uncertainty and the safety risks of stem cell medical tourism—traveling abroad for medical treatment—because stem cell treatments offer such amazing hope. Saenz says there is no way to stop people from wanting access to stem cell treatments,*

and until the United States begins offering them, people will do
whatever they have to do, including traveling to other countries,
to get them.

As you read, consider the following questions:

1. According to Saenz, what does the company Global Surgery Providers do?

2. How many people traveled outside the United States for medical treatment in 2007, according to the author?

3. According to Saenz, a JCI certificate is often seen as a guarantee of what?

You can't keep a good thing down. When the US restricted stem cell research in the early part of the century, that research didn't die, it emigrated. All over the world, scientists continued to explore the efficacies of embryonic and adult stem cells with astonishing results. Now, as the public becomes increasingly aware of these "miracle" treatments, the demand for stem cell therapies has increased far beyond what institutionalized Western medicine seems able to immediately provide. The result is both exhilarating and terrifying: more and more patients from the US and Europe are traveling abroad to seek stem cell treatments. This is just a tiny fraction of the ever increasing flood of medical tourism that has struck the West. Companies like Atlanta-based Global Surgery Providers (GSP) are marketing directly to patients, facilitating travel for medical procedures, including stem cell transplants. While governments, doctors, and patients are still struggling to understand the dangers and advantages of medical tourism, it continues to grow. One thing is for certain, no matter what any one institution may try to do to control the use of stem cells, the demand for this technology is too strong to be stopped.

US Roadblocks

While many researchers are working overtime to get stem cell therapies safely to market, the public perception in the US is that this technology is stalled. It doesn't help that big name studies, like the first US embryonic test by Geron, have run into bureaucratic roadblocks even after the political ones were pulled away. When the US allows stem cell treatments for animals, but not humans, this is seen as backwards, not as a necessary result of the stringent review applied to new medicine. It takes time for any new product to pass FDA [Food and Drug Administration] approval, but patients want stem cells *now*.

And why wouldn't they—have you seen some of the amazing things that stem cells can do? First there's the eye-popping pictures of new organs grown in labs. We've even seen a new windpipe created and implanted in just weeks thanks to a technique that used a patient's own stem cells. Add to that the promising results seen with diabetes and blindness—well, if I was in need of such a treatment, I would be demanding access to stem cells, too.

Medical Tourism

Which is where medical tourism comes in. Why wait years for the resolution of clinical trials and bureaucratic red tape when you can jump on a plane and get treated in a manner of weeks? Atlanta's GSP is just one of many medical travel agencies that has picked up on the stem cell trend. They offer consultations (via phone only at this time) that could help you find a stem cell therapy center somewhere across the world. Similar agencies cater to the UK, Canada, and many different locations in Europe.

When you see a company offering to take you to a foreign country for a miraculous new medical procedure, it can all seem new and untested. Parts of it are. Yet the medical tourism industry has been growing strong for years now. Once the province of cosmetic surgeries and dental procedures, medical tourism now includes those looking for hip/joint replacement, heart surgery, even organ transplants. Some 750,000 Americans were thought to have traveled outside the US for medical treatment in 2007. A survey published by Deloitte in 2009 found that 3% of those 3000 18- to 75-year-old Americans polled had used some form of medical tourism and that 27% would consider it. A significant 40% would pursue medical travel if they could save 50% or more on costs.

Cost and availability top the list of reasons why people seek healthcare travel. In the US, a heart valve operation might run you $200k, but the same procedure in India could be done for $10k, including travel and accommodations. In countries with socialized medicine, waiting for months on necessary (but not "critical") surgery pushes many to seek help outside their borders.

It's no wonder that different agencies have arisen to promote medical tourism and address the concerns of its detractors. The most well known of these is the Joint Commission International which seeks to certify hospitals and other medical facilities around the world. A JCI certificate is often seen as a guarantee that a facility will live up to Western medical standards. Other organizations, like the Medical Tourism Association, offer their own certification while serving as a business networking opportunity for those institutions that want to grow the industry.

Yet if medical tourism is increasingly seen as legitimate, "foreign" stem cell therapies are still stigmatized by the established medical profession. The International Society for Stem Cell Research (ISSCR) has called for greater transparency and open evaluation of stem cell therapies. They worry about clinics directly marketing to patients and using anecdotal evidence to support their medical claims. Even those medical travel agencies (like GSP) that are venturing into stem cell treatments are quick to advise patients that many treatments are untested, and that not all therapies will work for all people.

The problem with venturing outside the (painfully) slow review process that plagues the West is the presence of crippling uncertainty. For every clinic in Germany that seems to have somewhat reputable results, there's some clinic shut down in Hungary for being untested and unlicensed. Patients cannot know for sure if the treatments they receive as part of stem cell medical tourism will work. Or even be safe.

Patients Willing to Take Risks

I don't think that's going to stop anything. As I said in the beginning, you can't keep a good thing down. That's true even if you're uncertain about how good it really is. Stem cell therapies hold such amazing promise that they are going to be used no matter what. Years before the medical community as a whole would be comfortable with their use, stem cells have captured the hopes of patients the world over. In a sense, it doesn't matter if medical review processes are unnecessarily slow or not. It doesn't matter if stem cell therapies in different parts of the world are legitimate or not. Patients in need will seek out untested technologies as soon as the promised benefits outweigh the perceived risks. We've already passed that point. For better or for worse.

In a few years stem cell research is likely to be complete enough to produce clinically proven and nationally licensed therapies. But a few years can be a lifetime. I'm still doubtful as to whether stem cell clinics anywhere in the world really possess effective and safe treatments. Yet I know that dire situations force many to choose hope over doubt. Good luck to everyone, no matter which side of the coin you land on. And rest assured: one day recognized stem cell treatments will be available. Can't be stopped.

Periodical and Internet Sources Bibliography

The following articles have been selected to supplement the diverse views presented in this chapter.

Arthur Caplan — "The Stem Cell Hype Machine," *Science Progress*, March 18, 2011.

Stephen Cauchi — "Clone Rangers: Cell Scientists Tackle Balding One Hair at a Time," *Sydney Morning Herald (Australia)*, May 1, 2011.

Economist — "Science and Technology: A Strand Apart; Cancer and Stem Cells," January 16, 2010.

Kim Irwin — "Six UCLA Stem Cell Scientists Awarded More than $8 Million in State Grants," *UCLA Newsroom*, May 5, 2011.

Kim Kozlowski — "U-M Creates New Stem Cell Lines," *Detroit News*, April 4, 2011.

Robert Mendick and Allan Hall — "Europe's Largest Stem Cell Clinic Shut Down After Death of Baby," *Daily Telegraph (London)*, May 10, 2011.

Alan Mozes — "Scientists Use Stem Cells, Skin Cells to Create Brain Cells Lost to Alzheimer's," *U.S. News & World Report*, March 4, 2011.

Alice Park — "How Stem Cells Are Changing the Way We Think About Disease," *Time*, March 28, 2011.

Rob Stein — "First Patient to Get Stem Cell Therapy Comes Forward," *Washington Post*, April 7, 2011.

Rob Stein — "Scientists Overcome Hurdles to Stem Cell Alternatives," *Washington Post*, September 30, 2010.

OPPOSING
VIEWPOINTS®
SERIES

CHAPTER 2

Is Stem Cell Research Moral?

Chapter Preface

The word *chimera* comes from the name of the three-headed monster—lion, goat, and serpent—in Homer's *Iliad*. Chimeras, however, are not all monstrous or mythological. Scientists use the term to refer to a mixture of genetically distinct cells, which can come from the same or different species. Surprisingly, chimeras composed of cells from two different individuals of the same species are not uncommon in human biology. It is estimated that about 8 percent of nonidentical, or fraternal, twins have blood cells in their bodies that are from the other twin—making them chimeras. Chimerism also can occur in anyone who has a blood transfusion or an organ transplant. These are examples of chimerism between individuals, not between species.

Several decades ago, scientists began creating chimeras composed of cells from two different species in the laboratory. Interspecies chimeras include the geep, a chimera made by fusing a sheep embryo with a goat embryo, and the "quail-brained chicken," a quail-chicken chimera.

Since the late 1980s, scientists have also been injecting animals with human cells, creating human-animal chimeras. Stanford University professor Irving Weissman, while researching AIDS, was the first scientist to create a human-animal chimera. In 1988, along with his colleague Mike McCune, Weissman grafted adult human stem cells into a mouse lacking an immune system to create a mouse with a human immune system. This chimeric mouse allowed scientists to study the human immune system, and therefore AIDS, without using a human being.

Since then, scientists have created many other human-animal chimeras in the search for cures for neurological diseases, spinal cord injuries, diabetes, and other diseases.

For many years, chimera research did not attract a great deal of public attention; however, this started changing in the early twenty-first century—at the same time the country began debating the morality of human embryonic stem cell research. Weissman, who had moved on from creating mice with human immune systems to creating mice with human brain cells, explained in a July 2005 PBS interview that much of the interest in chimeras was due to the type of human cells being injected into animals, as well as the emergence of the embryonic stem cell debate:

> In the past the chimeric animals were mainly animals that we constructed with an organ that wasn't seemingly so important, skin, a bit of heart, a cancer. Now we're getting at the center of the issue, the brain, and since the brain, most of us believe, is the place where the human properties of mind, consciousness, learning, memory, emotion [reside], of course we should be interested in it. . . . I think that the issue of brain chimeras piggybacks on the whole issue of embryonic stem cell research, [the] nuclear transfer research that has politically divided the U.S.

While the objections to human embryonic stem cell research generally revolve around the destruction of human embryos and the question of when a developing human becomes a person, the debate about chimeras focuses on the ethics of blending animal cells with human cells—especially human brain cells. As Phillip Karpowicz, Cynthia Cohen, and Derek van der Kooy from the University of Toronto explain in a June 2005 essay in the *Kennedy Institute of Bioethics Journal*, "Stem cells associated with the brain seem to have a close association with what it is to be human. Such trans-species forays are disquieting because they would introduce human central nervous system stem cells into animals during their formative development when their future biological characteristics are beginning to emerge and before their body plans have been completed."

While the moral issues associated with chimera research are different from those associated with embryonic stem cell research, the two issues may soon merge. The US Food and Drug Administration generally requires that new medical treatments be tested on animals before they can be tested on humans. Many scientists think this will likely lead to a greater need for the creation of chimeras. In a May 2007 article in the *American Journal of Bioethics*, medical ethicists Henry Greely, Mildred Cho, Linda Hogle, and Debra Satz write, "The science and politics of human stem cells have combined to keep human/non-human chimeras a scientifically relevant issue. . . . As interest, scientific and popular, grows in human stem cell research, human/non-human chimeras are likely to take on broader uses."

The ethics of blending human and animal cells in the creation of chimeras is just one of the many moral issues associated with stem cell research. The authors of the viewpoints in the following chapter explore other moral questions surrounding stem cell research.

"If, as we believe, human embryos are human beings . . . then research that involves deliberately dismembering embryonic humans . . . is inherently wrong."

Embryonic Stem Cell Research Is Immoral Because Embryos Have Moral Status

Robert P. George and Patrick Lee

Robert P. George is the director of the James Madison Program in American Ideals and Institutions at Princeton University. Patrick Lee is the director of the Institute of Bioethics at the Franciscan University in Steubenville, Ohio. In the following viewpoint, George and Lee argue that embryos are human beings and have the same intrinsic worth as babies, children, and adults; therefore, they say, embryonic stem cell research that destroys embryos is immoral. George and Lee refute arguments that contend that embryos are not yet human or that embryos' lack of self awareness diminishes their moral standing. Whatever it is that gives each human being intrinsic moral worth, contend George and Lee, is present in an embryo just as it is in a child or an adult. Regardless of the manner in which they are brought into existence, whether naturally, by in vitro fertilization, or by cloning, embryos are human beings with full moral status, the authors maintain.

As you read, consider the following questions:

1. What does science writer Ronald Bailey compare embryos to, according to George and Lee?

2. According to the authors, the "sorites fallacy" assumes what?

3. According to George and Lee, who said that having a rational nature is a "status-conferring intrinsic property?"

If, as we believe, human embryos are human beings who deserve the same basic respect we accord to human beings at later developmental stages, then research that involves deliberately dismembering embryonic humans in order to use their cells for the benefit of others is inherently wrong. Just as harvesting the organs of a living child for the benefit of others is immoral and illegal, so 'disaggregating' embryonic human beings would also be immoral and should be illegal—of course governments should therefore not fund such procedures. In this article, we provide some of the evidence that human embryos are indeed human beings and, as such, deserve a level of respect that is incompatible with treating them as disposable research material. We also consider two recent objections to our position.

The Same as a Baby or Adult

In sexual reproduction, conception occurs when a sperm cell unites with an oocyte, the two cease to be, and their constituents successfully enter into the makeup of a new and distinct organism, which is called a zygote in its original one-celled stage. This new organism begins to grow by the normal process of differentiated cell division into an embryo, dividing into two cells, then four, eight and so on, although some divisions are asynchronous [not at the same time]. Its cells constitute a human organism, for they form a stable body and act together in a coordinated manner, which contributes to regular, predictable and determinate development toward the mature stage of a human being. That is, from the zygote stage onward, the human embryo has within it all of the internal information needed—including chiefly its genetic and epigenetic constitution—and the active disposition to develop itself to the mature stage of a human organism. As long as the embryo is reasonably healthy and is not denied or deprived of a suitable environment and adequate nutrition, it will actively develop itself along the species-specific trajectory of development. This means that the embryo has the same nature—in other words, it is the same kind of entity—from fertilization onward; there is only a difference in degree of maturation, not in kind, between any of the stages from embryo, to fetus, infant and so on. What exists in the early stages of development is not a mere bundle of homogeneous cells. Scientific evidence shows that already at the two-cell stage, and even more so at the four-cell stage and thereafter, there is a difference in the internal structure of the embryonic cells; although they have the same DNA, each has a distinct pattern of gene expression.

The human embryo is the same individual as the human organism at subsequent stages of development. The evidence for this is the genetic and epigenetic composition of this being—that is, the embryo's molecular composition is such that he or she has the internal resources to develop actively himself or herself to the next mature stage—and the typical embryo's regular, predictable and observable behaviour—that is, the embryo's actual progression through an internally coordinated and complex sequence of development to his or her mature stage.

It is important to note that embryological evidence shows that the human embryo is a whole, although obviously immature, human being; it is not a mere part. This is a crucial point: human tissues or human cells, whether body cells or gametes [reproductive cells] are indeed human—that is, genetically human—but are not whole human organisms. Neither of these has the active disposition to develop itself to the mature stage of a human being. By contrast, the human embryo, from fertilization onward, is fully programmed to actively develop himself or herself to the next mature stage along the path of human development.

More than Just Cells

One objection against this position is based on a comparison of human embryos to somatic cells [nonreproductive cells] given that producing humans by cloning is a possibility. Ronald Bailey, a science writer for *Reason* magazine, observes that each cell in the human body possesses the entire DNA code, but that each has become specialized as a muscle or skin cell, for example, by most of that code being turned off. During cloning, previously deactivated parts of the genome are reactivated. Bailey therefore argues that if human embryos are human beings with moral worth because of their potential to become adult humans, the same must be said of somatic cells, which is absurd.

However, Bailey's argument is based on a false analogy. The somatic cell is something from which a new organism can be generated; it is certainly not, however, a distinct organism. A human embryo, by contrast, is already a distinct, self-developing and complete human organism.

Moreover, the type of 'potentiality' possessed by somatic cells differs profoundly from the potentiality of the embryo. A somatic cell has a potential only in the sense that something can be done to it so that its constituents—its DNA molecules—enter into a distinct whole human organism, which is

Most Americans Have Not Considered the Morality of Embryo Research

For most Americans, the moral status of the human embryo is a question that seems quite remote. Even as hundreds of thousands of "excess" human embryos are now stored in American fertility clinics and laboratories, to most Americans these frozen embryos are out of sight and out of mind. Thus, one of the most important moral challenges of our day remains largely off the screen of our national discourse. The issue cannot remain out of sight or out of mind for long.

Albert Mohler,
AlbertMohler.com, August 28, 2009.

a human being, a person. In the case of the embryo, by contrast, he or she is already actively—indeed dynamically—developing himself or herself to the further stages of maturity of the human being he or she already is.

True, the whole genetic code is present in each somatic cell. However, this point fails to show that its potentiality is the same as that of a human embryo. When the nucleus of a somatic cell is inserted into an enucleated ovum [an egg cell with its nucleus removed] and given an electric stimulus, this is not merely the placing of the somatic cell into an environment hospitable to its continuing maturation and development. Rather, it generates a wholly distinct, self-integrating and entirely new organism—it generates an embryo. The entity—the embryo—brought into being by this process is radically different from the constituents that entered into its generation. . . .

Embryos Are Human Beings

Others have denied that human embryos are human beings, arguing that human beings come to be only gradually: human embryos are therefore on their way to becoming, but are not yet, human beings. This objection was advanced by Michael Sandel at Harvard University in his book *The Case Against Perfection*. According to Sandel, human organisms come to be gradually rather than at a determinate time, and a human organism is not fully present until some time after the embryonic stage. He states that this idea defeats the pro-human-embryo argument, which he recounts as follows: "the development of the embryo from the zygote stage on through the embryonic, fetal and infant stages is continuous, without any abrupt changes in direction of growth; therefore, one can conclude that there is no change in identity during that time, and, since a human infant is a human organism, so is a human zygote".

Sandel contends that this argument commits what philosophers know as the sorites fallacy; it illicitly assumes that one can never produce a radical change by the addition of several small changes. For example, suppose one reasoned as follows about grains of sand: "[w]e can never get a heap of sand from adding grains of sand to each other. For if I add just one grain to another that will not make a heap, and if I add another, that also will not produce a heap, since a tiny addition cannot change a few grains of sand into a heap. But the same point will be true for each grain of sand added, therefore I can never arrive at a heap of sand, by the repeated addition of a grain of sand to others." That is the sorites fallacy.

According to Sandel, the pro-human-embryo argument is therefore fallacious. From the fact that one cannot designate an instant or moment in which there is a radical change in the developmental process from a human embryo to a mature human being, it does not follow that there is no significant and radical difference between them. Consequently, Sandel argues, it does not follow that a human embryo is a human being. Rather, just as adding grains of sand to each other gradually produces something radically different, namely, a heap of sand, the process of development of the embryo and fetus in the womb gradually produces a human organism—but only gradually, not all at once.

Contrary to what Sandel assumes, however, the argument we presented above does not begin merely from the continuity of embryonic development. Sandel is of course right that the sorites fallacy is a fallacy—but he is mistaken in thinking that the basic pro-human-embryo argument commits it. The argument is not that an adult must be the same individual who was once an embryo simply because there is no significant difference between any two adjacent stages in the development from embryo to adult. Rather, the argument is that the adult is identical to the embryo he or she once was because there are no essential differences in the kind of being one is between any two stages—whether the two stages are adjacent to each other or not—in the development of a human individual from embryo to fetus, infant, child, adolescent and adult. There are of course several significant differences between an embryo, an infant and an adult—such as size and degree of development. But there is no difference in the kind—that is, there is no difference in the fundamental nature of the entity—between any two stages of the developing living being— whether those stages are adjacent to each other or are several months apart in his or her life cycle.

Again, the human embryo, from fertilization forward, develops in a single direction by an internally directed process: the developmental trajectory of this entity is determined from within, not by extrinsic factors, and always toward the same mature state, from the earliest stage of embryonic development onward. This means that the embryo has the same nature—it is the same kind of entity, a whole human organism—from fertilization forward; there is only a difference in degree of maturation between any of the stages in the development of the living being. . . .

All Human Beings Deserve Respect

Some grant that the human embryo is a human organism, but deny that this means it is a being deserving of full moral respect. They claim that in order to have dignity and a right to life, a human being must have additional characteristics such as self-awareness. Often this view is expressed along the following lines: "[w]hile human embryos are human organisms, they are not persons, and it is persons who deserve full moral respect, not necessarily human organisms."

We believe that this view, which relegates some living human beings to the status of 'non-persons', is profoundly mistaken. It is clear that one need not be actually or immediately conscious, reasoning, deliberating or making choices, in order to be a human being who deserves full moral respect, for plainly people who are asleep or in reversible comas deserve such respect. Thus, if one denies that human beings are intrinsically valuable by virtue of what they are, one requires an additional attribute, which must be a capacity of some type and, obviously, a capacity for certain mental functions.

Of course, human beings in the embryonic, fetal and early infant stages cannot yet exercise mental functions characteristically carried out by most human beings at later stages of maturity. Still, they have in radical—that is, root form—these very capacities. Precisely by virtue of the kind of entity they are, they are, from the beginning, actively developing themselves to the stages at which these capacities will—if all goes well—be immediately exercisable. Although, similar to infants, they have not yet developed themselves to the stage at which they are self-aware, it is clear that they are rational animal organisms. Having a rational nature is, in the words of Jeff McMahan at Rutgers University a "status-conferring intrinsic property". The argument is not that every member of the human species should be accorded full moral respect because the more mature members of the species have a status-conferring intrinsic property, as McMahan mistakenly interprets the nature-of-the-kind argument. Instead, we contend that each member of the human species has a rational nature.

It is obvious in practical deliberation that one's own well-being and fulfilment—such as one's own health and understanding—is worth pursuing and promoting. It is also obvious that the well-being and fulfilment of others is worth pursuing or at least respecting. However, the well-being and fulfilment of others is worthy of respect even at times when they are unconscious—when they are asleep, comatose or at any time that they exist, including those times during which they are developing to the stage at which they will be actually exercising the basic natural capacity for agency. We contend that these other entities are bearers of rights—their fulfilment is worthy of pursuit and respect, they should not be intentionally harmed, and they should be treated as we would have others treat us—because of the kind of entity they are, namely a creature with a rational nature, not in virtue of certain accidental characteristics such as age, size, location or stage of development. Briefly, we can advance two arguments to show that the substantial nature of the individual, and not accidental characteristics, should be recognized as the basis for having dignity and basic rights.

First, the developing human being does not reach a level of maturity at which he or she performs a type of mental act that other animals do not perform—even animals such as dogs and cats—until at least several months after birth. A 6-week-old baby cannot immediately perform characteristically human mental functions. However, if full moral respect were due only to those who have immediately exercisable capacities for characteristically human mental functions, it would follow that 6-week-old infants do not deserve full moral respect—some philosophers have actually claimed that infants do not deserve the moral respect of basic human rights. Thus, if human embryos might legitimately be destroyed to advance biomedical science, then it follows logically that, subject to parental approval, the body parts of human infants should be fair game for scientific experimentation.

Second, one might at first think that there are two types of capacity for consciousness or other mental functions: an immediately exercisable capacity for consciousness; and another, basic natural capacity that requires time and internal development in the organism before it can be actualized. One has this basic natural capacity for consciousness from the time that one comes to be—a human being has this capacity or potentiality from the embryonic stage forward by virtue of the fact that he or she has a disposition to actively develop to the stage where he or she will be conscious.

However, in reality, there is just one capacity for consciousness and just one capacity for each distinct type of living act. What is referred to as 'the immediately exercisable capacity' for consciousness is the development of that single capacity. A capacity such as that for consciousness is a power to perform a specific type of action. The capacity develops and comes closer to being the performance of that action, with the development of the constitution of the organism; however, in a living being, the transition from the basic natural capacity to perform an action characteristic of living beings on the one hand, to the performance of that action on the other hand, is just the development of the basic power that the organism has from its beginning. The capacity for consciousness is gradually developed or brought towards maturation, through gestation, childhood, adolescence and so on.

Proponents of an immediately exercisable capacity for mental functions as a criterion for having dignity and a right to life do not select one property or feature rather than another as a criterion for dignity and rights. Instead, they select a certain degree of a property. However, such a selection is inevitably arbitrary. For why should the *n*th degree of that property qualify one as having rights? Why not the *n*th + 1 degree or the *n*th + 2 degrees and so on? The difference between a being that deserves full moral respect and a being that does not—and might therefore legitimately be killed to benefit others—cannot consist only of the fact that, while both have some feature, one has more of it than the other—one has some arbitrarily selected degree of the development of some feature or property, whereas the other does not. This conclusion would follow no matter which of the acquired qualities proposed as qualifying some human beings or human beings at some developmental stages for full respect were selected.

Embryos Are Worthy of Respect

The criterion we propose—that of a creature being an individual with a rational nature—does not suffer from this problem of arbitrariness. There is a radical difference between individuals with a rational nature and other entities, and that difference is morally relevant—rational creatures, at all times that they exist, should be treated as we would have others treat us.

It follows that it cannot be the case that some human beings and not others are intrinsically valuable, by virtue of a certain degree of development. Rather, human beings are intrinsically valuable in the way that allows us to ascribe to them equality and basic rights in virtue of what they are; and all human beings are intrinsically valuable.

As human beings are intrinsically valuable and deserve full moral respect in virtue of what they are, it follows that they are intrinsically and equally valuable from the point at which they come into being. Even in the embryonic stage of our lives, each of us was a human being and, as such, worthy of concern and protection. Embryonic human beings, whether brought into existence by the union of gametes, somatic-cell nuclear transfer or other cloning technologies, should be accorded the respect given to human beings in other developmental stages. Their right to life should be acknowledged and respected.

"We should never create or destroy embryos lightly. We owe them our respect. We just don't owe them the same respect we owe one another."

Embryos Do Not Have the Same Moral Status as People

William Saletan

William Saletan writes the Human Nature column for Slate *and is the author of* Bearing Right: How Conservatives Won the Abortion War. *In the following viewpoint, Saletan contends that embryos are not morally equivalent to people. He evaluates the 2008 book* Embryo *by Robert George and Christopher Tollefsen, which uses science to argue that personhood begins at conception. According to Saletan, George and Tollefsen's argument falls apart upon a close examination of the science behind human conception and development. Identifying the absolute moment personhood begins, says Saletan, is just as difficult in scientific terms as it is in ethical terms. Saletan contends that embryos have moral worth, but he does not argue that they have the same worth that living human beings possess.*

As you read, consider the following questions:

1. According to Saletan, if embryos are morally equal to people, then extracting a single cell from a very early embryo is a violation of what?

2. What does the author say is the "congenial environment" described by George and Tollefsen?

3. According to Saletan, scientists theorize that "reproductive plasticity" is designed to do what in some species?

Thirty-five years after *Roe v. Wade* [the 1973 Supreme Court decision that granted women the right to obtain abortions legally], the pro-life movement faces a new challenge: biotechnology. The first human biotech issue, embryonic stem-cell research, looks like an easy call. Stem cells could save millions of lives. And the entity we currently sacrifice to get them—a sacrifice that may soon be unnecessary—is a tiny, undeveloped ball of cells. The question, like the embryo, seems a no-brainer.

For pro-lifers, that's precisely the problem. Biotechnology is arguably more insidious than abortion. Abortions take place one at a time and generally as a response to an accident, lapse or nasty surprise. Their gruesomeness actually limits their prevalence by arousing revulsion and political opposition. Conventional stem-cell harvesting is quieter but bolder. It's deliberate and industrial, not accidental and personal. In combination with cloning, it entails the mass production, exploitation and destruction of human embryos. Yet its victims don't look human. You can't protest outside a fertility clinic waving a picture of a blastocyst. You have to explain what it is and why people should care about it.

A Risky Argument

This is the task Robert George and Christopher Tollefsen undertake in *Embryo*. To reach a secular and skeptical public, they avoid religion and stake their case on science. George, a professor of jurisprudence at Princeton and a member of the President's Council on Bioethics, and Tollefsen, a philosopher at the University of South Carolina, locate humanity not in a soul but in a biological program. "To be a complete human organism," they write, "an entity must possess a developmental program (including both its DNA and epigenetic factors) oriented toward developing a brain and central nervous system." The program begins at conception; therefore, so does personhood.

The argument's absolutism is crucial. In the last three months [December 2007–February 2008], scientists have announced two ways to get stem cells without killing embryos. One method is to extract a single cell from the very early embryo. The other is to reprogram adult cells to make them embryonic. But if embryos are morally equal to people, then the first method violates patient consent and the second leaves unresolved crises in embryo research and in vitro fertilization [I.V.F.]. George and Tollefsen would ban research that poses even slight risks to an embryo's health. They would abolish production of spare I.V.F. embryos and require every fertilized embryo to be transferred to a womb.

The argument is brave but risky. Shifting the pro-life case from religion to science puts it at the mercy of scientific discovery, with all the attendant surprises. Indeed, the human program turns out to be quite complicated. It discredits the authors' absolutism.

The Science Defies the Argument

George and Tollefsen reason that the embryo is fully human and its life therefore inviolable, because its program is self-contained. "Nothing extrinsic to the developing organism itself acts on it to produce a new character or new direction of growth," they write. The embryo has all the "structures necessary for providing the new individual with a suitable environ-

Full-Fledged *and* Potential

I would describe the traditional Jewish approach to pre-birth life as follows: an embryo and fetus are full-fledged human lives *and* they are potential lives. In other words, embryonic and fetal life are worthy of protection, since they are human lives. But they are *also* potential lives whose existence as persons does not become fully established until birth. Accordingly, they are not afforded the *same* protection that born humans receive. The blood of fetuses and embryos is *not* quite as red as that of those who've been born.

Michael Rosen, Ideas in Action,
October 6, 2005. www.ideasinactiontv.com.

ment and adequate nutrition." It can "get itself to the uterus," "burrow" into the uterine wall and begin "taking in nourishment" from "a congenial environment."

Nobody with a womb would describe pregnancy this way. The "congenial environment" is a woman. The embryo doesn't "get itself" around her like some Horatio Alger hero. Her body sustains it, guides it and affects its direction of growth. Mother and child are a system.

While quoting from embryology textbooks, the authors omit passages that confound their bootstrap theory. One such passage reports that "the early embryo and the female reproductive tract influence one another" as the embryo is "being transported" to the uterus. Another observes that "implantation requires a high degree of preparation and coordination by both the embryo and the endometrium"—preparation that begins, on the womb's part, well before conception. Maternal factors don't just facilitate the embryo's program; they direct it. Maternal RNA guides the embryo's early organization. Later, factors in the womb apparently influence traits like sexual orientation.

Life's program precedes, succeeds and transcends the individual. Hence the old riddle of which came first, the chicken or the egg. Everything overlaps. Within two weeks of conception, a female embryo's primordial germ cells begin the assembly of her future children. Her primary oocytes [egg cells] are complete at birth. The embryo is already maternal.

The authors think this unfolding trajectory justifies an equation of embryos with adults. "The proper way to identify the nature of an organism," they write, is "to look at it through time." Each of us "comes into existence as a single-celled human organism and develops, if all goes well, into adulthood." But in the big picture, the embryo isn't a future adult. It is, as the authors acknowledge, a future corpse. And the program is far bigger. It doesn't end at death, because it doesn't run on one body. It runs on the network of humanity. In fact, it runs on the entire Internet of evolving species.

The program's collective nature doesn't discredit individual rights. But it does complicate the authors' task. They have to show that the embryo is an individual, not just a program. Here, again, science defies them. They write that the embryo's cells "function together to develop into a single, more mature member of the human species." Not quite. In one of every 300 cases, the embryo splits to become two or more people, at least one of whom wasn't a distinct organism at conception. And in every case, part of the embryo becomes placenta, nurturing the other part and passing away. The embryo, too, is collective.

Drawing Moral Lines Is Difficult

The authors think a clear line can be drawn between eggs, which are parts of organisms, and embryos, which are wholes. Eggs must combine with sperm or die, they write, and an organism "was never itself a sperm cell or an ovum." But science tells another story. In some 70 vertebrate species, unfertilized eggs have developed into offspring. A United States government report documents dozens of mature turkeys that were never fathered. This, too, is part of life's program. Scientists call it "reproductive plasticity." In some species, they theorize, it's designed to pass on genes when no mates are available. If the egg-embryo distinction gets in the way, nature suspends it.

Technology further muddles the embryo's boundaries. In vitro fertilization separates the internal and external portions of the embryonic program. Cloning turns adult body cells into embryos. Direct reprogramming turns body cells into embryonic stem cells. Aggregation turns embryonic mouse stem cells into mice. Altered nuclear transfer, which the authors encourage, causes ingredients that would otherwise become an embryo to become instead a mess of stem cells. The difference is a single gene.

None of these confounding discoveries destroy the book's essential and timely message. Of all the lines we could draw in human development to mark the onset of moral worth, conception is the brightest. But that line is no more absolute in ethics than in science. We should never create or destroy embryos lightly. We owe them our respect. We just don't owe them the same respect we owe one another.

> *"This marked lack of curiosity about what is claimed to be of immense importance [embryonic life] suggests that even now, few people really believe that full moral status begins at conception."*

The Moral Argument Against Embryonic Stem Cell Research Is Flawed

Toby Ord

Toby Ord is a philosopher at the University of Oxford and the director of Giving What We Can, a society that helps fight global poverty. In the following viewpoint, Ord asserts that the argument that embryos have the same moral status as born human beings is flawed. According to Ord, if one believes that embryos have the same moral status as living people, than one must be horrified by the number of embryos that die naturally within the first few weeks after conception. However, according to Ord, people who oppose embryonic stem cell research because it harms days-old embryos do not seem to be alarmed at the number of embryos lost to spontaneous abortion. Ord argues that this means that most people really do not believe that embryos have the same moral status as living people.

As you read, consider the following questions:

1. What percentage of embryos successfully implant, according to Ord?

2. As reported by the author, how many people are killed by cancer worldwide each year versus the number of embryos killed by spontaneous abortion?

3. Ord mentions a call to arms that followed the publication of what book?

The Scourge struck swiftly and brutally. This terrifying new disease, more deadly than any before it, left no part of the world untouched. From the poorest countries in Africa to the richest countries of the West, it killed with equal, horrifying, efficiency. It struck quickly, killing most of its victims within a few weeks of onset, and silently, for there were no detectable symptoms prior to death. Before the Scourge, the global death rate was 55 million per annum. That is, all causes of death—old age, war, murder, disease, and so on—conspired to take 55 million lives each year. The Scourge changed this dramatically. It alone killed more than 200 million people every year. From that time on, more than three quarters of the deaths each year were due to the Scourge. Where life expectancy in the West had risen steadily over the past century to 78 years, it had now dropped to just 29. Perhaps worst of all, the effects of the Scourge were not felt equally across all members of society. It killed only the very young and innocent—those who were completely powerless to prevent it.

Compared with the Scourge, all other problems seemed insignificant. The Scourge was the major issue of the age, and there was an overwhelming obligation on society to fight it.

Other projects had to be put on hold and a major international effort directed towards loosening the Scourge's grip upon humanity.

The Scourge is a fiction, but a telling one. There is a very common claim made in reproductive ethics: that the human embryo has full moral status. This claim is of pivotal importance in the abortion debate, and it thus has a strong influence over the political landscape in the United States (US) and elsewhere. However, if this claim is true, then we are already facing a threat as dire as the Scourge.

We shall begin with an explanation of the ethical claim that an embryo has full moral status. We shall then examine a rarely discussed fact about human embryology and show how, in combination with the ethical claim, this leads directly to an astounding conclusion which few people will be prepared to accept. This leaves proponents of the claim with a stark choice: they must either endorse this unwelcome conclusion, or give up the claim and lose the support that it lent to their positions on abortion, *in vitro* fertilization (IVF) and stem cells.

The Claim

The ethical debates around abortion, IVF, and the procurement of human embryonic stem cells all depend on the moral status of the human embryo. Opponents of these practices frequently claim that embryos have full moral status from the moment of conception. That is, from the time when the ovum is fertilized, the resulting embryo has the same moral status as an adult human being. For brevity, we can call this *the Claim.*

Proponents of the Claim argue that it would be impermissible to destroy an adult human being in order to achieve the benefits of abortion, IVF, or stem cell use, and thus it would also be impermissible to destroy an embryo for these purposes. If the Claim were false, and embryos had a lower moral status than adult humans, then it would be much more diffi-cult to reach such conclusions. Thus, much of the debate turns on the truth of the Claim.

In explaining the position of the Catholic Church, Nick Tonti-Filippini gives a typical statement of the Claim:

> The Church sees every human life at every stage as equally worthy of protection and the more vulnerable a human be-ing is at a particular stage, the more strenuous should be the community's efforts to protect him or her. . . . Thus from that first moment, that new human being demands the un-conditioned respect that is morally due to a human being in his or her bodily and spiritual totality.

This full moral status need not always entail equal treatment, for in some cases the differences in circumstances between an adult human and an embryo would be pertinent. For ex-ample, we do not need to defend an embryo's right to free speech because it cannot yet communicate. However, full moral status does entitle an entity to equal consideration: it implies that we must give the interests of embryos full weight in our ethical decision making. Because embryos have as much to lose from being destroyed as adult humans do, we would be required to refrain from killing them when we ought not kill an adult human and to protect their lives when we would be required to protect the life of an adult human.

Note that the Claim is not simply that the embryo is a hu-man being. This would merely be a biological classification and would have no direct ethical import. It is often used as a stepping-stone to the Claim ('embryos are human beings; all human beings have equal moral status; therefore embryos have full moral status') but it is perfectly possible to accept that embryos are human beings without according them full moral status.

The purpose of this article is to show that the Claim leads to a very troubling conclusion. For the sake of argument, we

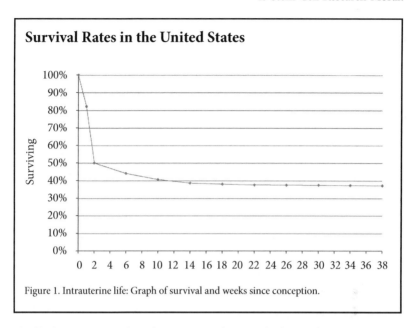

Figure 1. Intrauterine life: Graph of survival and weeks since conception.

shall thus accept that human embryos *do* have full moral status from the moment of conception and show where this leads us.

Natural Embryo Loss

The majority of embryos die within a few weeks of conception. This fact is widely known within medical circles, but is a surprise to many in the general public. Embryo death due to natural causes is known as *spontaneous abortion* and occurs very frequently. Two of the most respected studies of the incidence of spontaneous abortion are by [embryologist, Arthur] Hertig and by [public health physicians, Fern] French and [Jesse] Bierman. The information from these was combined by [French demographer Henri] Leridon in the form of an intrauterine life table (represented in Figure 1).

As Figure 1 shows, the riskiest time is before the embryo has implanted in the uterine wall (which typically occurs between 8 to 10 days after conception. During this early stage, the proportion of surviving embryos drops off rapidly and only approximately 50% of them successfully implant. For

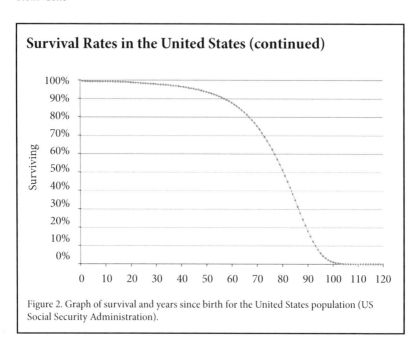

Figure 2. Graph of survival and years since birth for the United States population (US Social Security Administration).

those embryos that do implant successfully, the risk of death becomes much less significant and most will survive through to term.

These numbers show that spontaneous abortion is an everyday phenomenon. A mother of three children could be expected to have also had approximately five spontaneous abortions. An embryo's survival to term is the exception rather than the norm.

It might seem surprising that these dramatic death rates for early embryos could remain unknown to the general public. However, the reason for this is that most embryo loss occurs before the pregnancy has been detected, and the woman is unaware that anything out of the ordinary has happened. The embryo simply passes out of the uterus with the next menses.

Life tables such as that represented in Figure 1 show the decline in the size of a population over time. They allow us to see the proportion of the population surviving at any particular time and to ascertain where the significant rates of death

Survival Rates in the United States (continued)

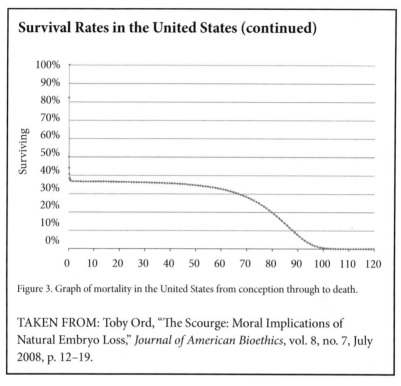

Figure 3. Graph of mortality in the United States from conception through to death.

TAKEN FROM: Toby Ord, "The Scourge: Moral Implications of Natural Embryo Loss," *Journal of American Bioethics*, vol. 8, no. 7, July 2008, p. 12–19.

occur. The most familiar type of life table shows a population from birth until an age where all members have died. For example, Figure 2 is a chart of the 2002 life table for the US [from the US Social Security Administration].

The curve begins with a distinct drop in the first year, which corresponds to the small, but noticeable, level of infant mortality in the developed world. Then comes a very gradual decline, which becomes steeper after middle age, drops quickly from age 70 through to 90 years, and then levels off once more. The point where the curve crosses the 50th percentile gives the median lifespan of 80 years. In this case it corresponds quite closely with the mean lifespan (or life expectancy) of 78 years.

Now let us join Figures 1 and 2—the unfamiliar and the familiar—to form the complete representation of mortality in the United States, from conception through to death (Figure 3).

This graph shows a very different view of human mortality. Here again is the familiar S-curve that shows the totality of deaths since birth. That smooth decline includes all deaths due to war, murder, disease and accident. However, all of this is overshadowed by the initial precipitous drop due to spontaneous abortion. In those first few months, more than 60% of the entire population die. For those who accept the Claim, each of these deaths (of which there are 220 million per year) must have just as much weight as the death of an adult human. For them, spontaneous abortion is the greatest killer of all: it is the Scourge.

An Unwelcome Conclusion

If we compare the description of the Scourge to the facts relating to spontaneous abortion we are faced with the following:

- Both are more deadly than anything else in human history.

- Both strike with equal effect in all parts of the world.

- Both kill most of their victims within weeks of onset.

- Neither is detectable before death occurs.

- Both kill more than 200 million people each year.

- Both account for more than three quarters of all deaths per year.

- Both reduce the life expectancy in the developed world to a mere 29 years.

- Both kill the very young and innocent: those who are powerless to save themselves.

The only differences are that the Scourge was said to be a disease and that it arrived suddenly. Spontaneous abortion has not arrived suddenly: it has been with us since humanity arose. It is not a disease, but a label that applies to all embryo death from natural causes. Those differences gave the Scourge a sense of immediacy, but were not ethically relevant. That cancer has been with us since the earliest days does not make it any less bad, or reduce the need for a cure. That spontaneous abortion is caused by a variety of genetic and hormonal problems does not make it any less bad either.

What is relevant is that (according to the Claim) it leads to more regrettable human death than all other causes put together. Cancer, in all its forms, kills 7.6 million people per year, while spontaneous abortion kills 30 times this number [according to the World Health Organization]. In 6 years, the Second World War killed approximately 60 million people, whereas spontaneous abortion kills more than three times this number every year. For supporters of the Claim there is little choice but to see it as one of the world's greatest problems, if not *the* greatest problem.

The introduction to the Scourge ended with a practical conclusion:

> There was an overwhelming obligation on society to fight it. Other projects had to be put on hold and a major international effort directed towards loosening the Scourge's grip upon humanity.

For supporters of the Claim, it is difficult to resist a similar conclusion. Finding means of saving even 5% of embryos from spontaneous abortion would save more lives than a cure for cancer. If we see one of these as requiring an immense international collaboration, then why not the other?

The Conclusion Based on the Claim

The argument then, is as follows. The embryo has the same moral status as an adult human (the Claim). Medical studies show that more than 60% of all people are killed by spontaneous abortion (a biological fact). Therefore, spontaneous abortion is one of the most serious problems facing humanity, and we must do our utmost to investigate ways of preventing this death—even if this is to the detriment of other pressing issues (the Conclusion).

I do not expect many people to accept the Conclusion. Instead, most of the people who see this argument say that the Conclusion is absurd: that it may be somewhat regrettable for so many embryos to die, but it is certainly not one of the world's major issues. Indeed, I too share this response. However, this is not compatible with accepting the Claim. For the argument shows that when combined with an important medical fact, the Claim leads immediately to the highly dubious Conclusion.

Is there any way out of this for defenders of the Claim? One certainly *could* save the Claim by embracing the Conclusion; however, I doubt that many of its supporters would want to do so. Instead, I suspect that they would either try to find some flaw in the argument, or abandon the Claim. Even if they were personally prepared to embrace the Conclusion, the Claim would lose much of its persuasive power. Many of the people they were trying to convince are likely to see the Conclusion as too bitter a pill, and to decide that if these embryo-related practices are wrong at all, it cannot be due to the embryo having full moral status.

This argument, in its basic form, is not original to the present paper. Since the writing of this paper, I have found similar arguments advanced by [Timothy] Murphy, [Peter] Millican and [Ronald] Green, who appear to have arrived at it independently. However, none of them seem to realize quite how far the argument can be taken: Millican and Green spend only a few sentences discussing it, whereas Murphy provides a fuller treatment, but does not reach as strong a formulation of the Conclusion and is thus hesitant to treat it as more than an interesting consequence of the Claim. Only in his final remarks does Murphy venture that the Conclusion is 'problematic'.

Because it has not been put in its strongest terms, the argument has not received its due attention. The argument is medically and philosophically simple. It shows a highly suspect conclusion that can be derived directly from one of the core bio-conservative claims. It is a pressing concern for all people who are moved to ban abortion, IVF, or the gathering of stem cells, on the grounds that the embryo has full moral status since the time of conception.

This argument is distinct from a number of other arguments that appeal to the rates of spontaneous abortion. For example, it is sometimes said that since so many embryos die naturally, IVF and stem cell research are at least as ethical as natural reproduction; or, since so many embryos die naturally, we would have an obligation to take a pill to avoid spontaneous abortion if such a pill were available; or, since so many embryos die naturally, the Claim would make it wrong to conceive; or even since so many embryos die naturally, it doesn't matter if we kill one.

Some of these other arguments have merit and some do not. Either way, they should not be confused with the argument being made here, which is that since so many embryos die naturally, the Claim would oblige us to treat this as one of the world's most serious problems and direct truly significant resources towards saving them. . . .

Implications

To many, the Conclusion is completely implausible. They find widespread embryo death to be surprising and perhaps regrettable, but certainly not a key moral issue of our time. I will not argue directly for the falsity of the Conclusion here, but rather will let its implausibility speak for itself. Some, no doubt, will defend the Conclusion, but most people will find it preposterous.

The only way to avoid the Conclusion is to abandon the Claim—to accept that full moral status does not begin at con-

Embryos Are Not Persons

It is implausible . . . that anything that deserves the name of a person could warrant as little moral consideration as we give either to human embryos in hypothetical embryo-rescue cases or to spontaneous abortion. It seems unlikely, for example, that we could be indifferent to any disease that killed 220 million people per year, even if it affected only the very old. Moreover, even if we did tolerate the deaths of 220 million people from disease, we would nevertheless take great cognisance of those deaths, and would accord the dead the dignity of the same burial rituals that we accord to others. Neither of these seems to be required in the case of early spontaneous abortion. The only viable option is to accept that embryos are not persons; hence, the claim that they are persons has no place in the debate on whether unwanted embryos might be destroyed in research.

Thomas Douglas and Julian Savulescu,
EMBO Reports, *2009.*

ception. This will seriously undermine the most prominent objections to induced abortion, IVF, and the collection of stem cells. If these practices are wrong at all, then it must be for some other reason. Opponents of these practices who formerly accepted the Claim will have to re-evaluate the situation, for they cannot consistently remain opposed without new arguments. Whether they eventually change their minds on these practices or not, they will have to join others in one of the most difficult ventures of reproductive ethics: finding a non-arbitrary time after conception at which full moral status is first attained.

Does this argument have any impact for those who already think that the embryo has partial status? It depends upon the exact position. For example, those who grant the embryo full moral status *in utero*, but lesser status if removed prior to development, are vulnerable to exactly the same argument. If the embryo has full moral status *in utero*, then we would have an overwhelming duty to protect all those embryos which spontaneously abort. In general, if an embryo is granted sufficient moral status in the first few weeks of a pregnancy to require active protection when threatened, then the Conclusion will follow.

Those who 'bite the bullet' and accept the Conclusion will have a very difficult time. They will have to accept a very strange ethical belief, and they cannot leave it as a purely theoretical view—for if they really believe that the Scourge is with us, then they will be compelled to fervent action. It is also a belief that will alienate them from much of the public. It will be very difficult to convince people that the Claim makes induced abortion wrong when they know that the Claim comes along with the Conclusion.

Finally, it is worth reflecting on the very simplicity of the argument. The Claim is widely held. The medical fact is not widely known to the general public, but is hardly a secret. Surely many of those who truly consider embryos to be the moral equal of adult humans would want to investigate the health of embryos and would find the statistics on spontaneous abortion. The Conclusion then directly follows from the Claim and these statistics.

A true believer in the Claim should be deeply interested in the terrifying Conclusion and should act to alert others to the existence of this Scourge. We might expect something like the call to arms following the publication of *Animal Liberation*. However, there has been no such call from the proponents of the Claim. Even if they had an objection to the argument, it would be of grave importance to make sure that this objection really works and that the argument does not go through. It could not be enough to merely reach personal satisfaction on the matter, for with 200 million lives per year at stake, it would surely be a matter for heated discussion in the journals or in the Church. This marked lack of curiosity about what is claimed to be of immense importance suggests that even now, few people really believe that full moral status begins at conception.

> *"The era of the embryo 'wars' may be coming to an end."*

The Debate About Embryos and Stem Cell Research May Be Coming to an End

Arthur L. Caplan and Pasquale Patrizio

Arthur L. Caplan is a professor of bioethics and the director of the Center for Bioethics at the University of Pennsylvania. Pasquale Patrizio is a professor of obstetrics, gynecology, and reproductive sciences and the clinical practice director at the Yale University Fertility Center. In the following viewpoint, Caplan and Patrizio contend that the American and world public is forming a consensus about the moral status of embryos. According to Caplan and Patrizio, public understanding about natural embryo loss and differences in the survivability of embryos, as well as a rejection of the claim that a moral line cannot be drawn between embryos and adults, are leading to the consensus. Caplan and Patrizio believe that there are huge areas of agreement concerning the creation and use of embryos in therapy and research.

Arthur L. Caplan and Pasquale Patrizio, "The Beginning of the End of the Embryo Wars," *The Lancet*, vol. 373, no. 9669, March 28–April 3, 2009, pp. 1074–1075. Copyright © 2009, Elsevier. All rights reserved. Reproduced by permission.

As you read, consider the following questions:

1. As cited by Caplan and Patrizio, what is the name of the doctrine that makes it clear that the Roman Catholic Church is committed to the belief that all human embryos are full members of the human community?

2. According to Caplan and Patrizio, of embryos attained through assisted reproduction, what percentage on average lead to a live birth?

3. What position, although argued fervently by those who believe in the equality of embryos, does Caplan and Patrizio think makes little sense metaphysically or ethically?

It is hard to remember a time when more attention has been paid to the moral status of the human embryo. This is strange since human embryos have been known to scientists and, shortly thereafter, to theologians, philosophers, and everyone else since at least the 19th century. It is not at all strange in another sense, since scientists have been unwilling to venture into the domain of specifying what the moral status of a human embryo might be. Some of that reluctance is perhaps ill-advised, because empirical information is having a perspicuous effect on key dimensions of this moral quandary.

Embryos the Center of Attention

Whatever human embryos are, and whatever ethical stance adult humanity ought to adopt towards them, in recent years embryos have not wanted for publicity. Human embryos, the headlines blare, have been: cloned from adult skin cells, created from the genetic material of three people, key players in a lawsuit where preimplantation genetic testing failed to detect and thus prevent a terrible congenital form of cancer, and sorted to prevent the occurrence of an early form of breast cancer. Embryos have also been making headlines as the subjects of a worldwide effort to find ways to avoid destroying them to generate stem cells.

Lawmakers also have embryos on their minds. President [Barack] Obama, with great fanfare and praise, as well as a bit of moral derision from some quarters, recently declared that public funds would, contrary to the policy of his predecessor, be available for embryonic stem cell research in the USA. Other solons [lawgivers] have enacted or proposed legislation that would require the consent of donors before any research could be done on stem cells produced via nuclear transfer cloning; permit the creation of human-animal hybrid embryos for research; compel the listing of unwanted embryos as "adoptable" at in-vitro fertilisation clinics; and mandated that all embryos created in in-vitro fertilisation be implanted.

Recent efforts to create moral equality between human embryos and the rest of us have found support in various religious teachings. This concern is much in evidence, for example, in the important instruction offered by the Vatican's Congregation for the Doctrine of the Faith, *Dignitas Personae*. This teaching, issued with the explicit approval of the Pope, makes it very clear that the Roman Catholic Church remains unwavering in its moral commitment to include all human embryos as full members of the human community.

And it is not just theologians who have put the embryo at the centre of the ethical stage. A tide of publications, opinion pieces, and editorials have appeared over the past few years that try to secure a secular basis for the view that human embryos ought be accorded full moral standing. Ballot initiatives, governmental directives, and legislation that would grant embryos personhood have also popped into prominent view in the USA and Italy.

Points of Consensus

The war over the moral standing of the embryo is as heated and contentious as it ever has been. Yet, despite the appearance of much florid verbiage to the contrary, the era of the embryo "wars" may be coming to an end.

How can this be? In the USA alone political discourse in national, state, and local elections has been embryocentric for years. Similarly, battles over the morality of embryo destruction, the manipulation of embryos in research, the creation of chimeric embryos, and the cloning of embryos have dominated the headlines and occupied the attention of commissions, clergy, and committees in the UK, the European Union, South Korea, Italy, Japan, Canada, Australia, Germany, Spain, Israel, Brazil, Sweden, South Africa, Poland, and Singapore for just as long. There would seem to be nothing but a continued storm of controversy on the intellectual horizon when matters turn to how we ought to value and interact with human embryos.

If one looks a bit more closely though there are signs that the debate over the status, creation, use, and disposition of human embryos has peaked. Some points of ethical consensus have begun to emerge both about the moral standing of embryos and what can be done with them.

One point of consensus is that not all embryos are morally equal. Partly this is due to the increasing knowledge we have from medicine and science about human embryos. It has become increasingly clear that most embryos—more than 80%—produced in vitro and transferred into the uterus during assisted reproductive treatments lack any capacity for development under any circumstances due to chromosomal or genetic defects. An embryo obtained through assisted reproduction has a very small chance of leading to a live birth, with only 15% of embryos on average developing into an infant. The knowledge that an embryo developed in vitro has only a minimal potential for life has shed considerable and penetrating light on the claim that every embryo must be regarded as a person and on the ethical discussion involving the handling of unwanted or surplus embryos.

The extent to which embryo loss is a natural phenomenon of human sexual reproduction has also shifted opinion about the moral status of human embryos. Although it is true that every life begins with the conception of a human embryo, it is now understood to be far from true that every conception of an embryo initiates a human life. The facts of human embryonic development in nature and in the laboratory undercut the claims both that all embryos are created equally and as adult humanity's moral equals.

Circumstances Matter

Distinctions are also starting to emerge between the creation of human embryos for the purpose of research and for the purpose of reproduction. Many who would assign full moral standing to every embryo from the moment of conception believe that the creation and destruction of embryos in the context of in-vitro fertilisation is ethically wrong. That view, however, remains a distinctly minority point of view.

Using in-vitro fertilisation to assist infertile people in the creation of children, despite the large number of human embryos lost, has elicited hardly any efforts at criminalisation or prohibition. And in looking at the policies adopted by many nations, it is clear that using "surplus" embryos that were initially created with the intent of turning them into babies at infertility clinics, but which could not be so used, for adoption or (far more likely) research has gained enormous ethical support. Embryos created with the goal of reproduction but that are no longer going to be used for that purpose face only one likely fate—destruction. This being so, making them available for research seems to many to be an act of moral redemption akin to procuring organs from a dead body. The fact that catastrophic circumstance caused the death does not as a matter of public policy preempt obtaining organs and tissues to help others.

Majority of Americans Think Embryonic Stem Cell Research Is Morally Acceptable

Next, I'm going to read you a list of issues. Regardless of whether or not you think it should be legal, for each one, please tell me whether you personally believe that in general it is morally acceptable or morally wrong. How about medical research using stem cells obtained from human embryos?

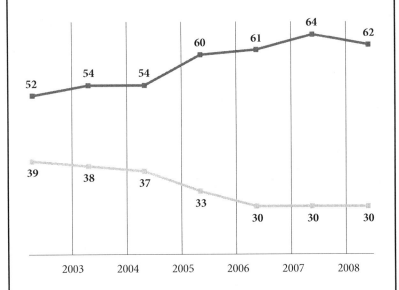

■ % Morally acceptable

▨ % Morally wrong

TAKEN FROM: Lyman Morales, "Majority of Americans Likely Support Stem Cell Decision," *Gallup*, March 9, 2009.

Similarly, the permissibility of destroying unclaimed frozen embryos after a reasonable period of time has gained much worldwide acceptance. And the moral propriety of creating human embryos via cloning for research as well as the morality of preimplantation diagnosis of embryos in order to avoid fatal or severely disabling illness have also secured widespread acceptance. A handful of nations still restrict embryo destruction. But, even so countries such as Italy, which permits preimplantation genetic diagnosis but then requires that even if an embryo is found to carry a lethal or severely disabling disease that it must be transferred and cannot be discarded, nonetheless permit the termination of the pregnancy if the fetus is later found to have a severely disabling disease.

The push to grant embryos equivalent moral standing to adult human beings has not succeeded in most parts of the world. For example, legislative efforts to assign personhood to the embryo from the moment of conception have consistently gone down to defeat in the USA and elsewhere.

Reasons for Agreement

Why is this so? Interestingly enough, the reason that the embryo debate has peaked is that the public has heard the key claims made by proponents of embryo equality and, over time, has not been persuaded as to their validity. There is a growing understanding of empirical facts about differences among embryos and the rate at which they fail to develop in nature and in the laboratory leading to the rejection of claims about the universal moral status of all human embryos. The relevance these facts have played in shifting public opinion should give the lie to the view that science has nothing to contribute to normative discussions about the status and use of human embryos. But, it is not just a growing appreciation of the facts that has weakened the case for granting all human embryos moral equivalence with the rest of us.

The public also has rejected normative claims that hold that since it is hard to draw a distinct demarcation in the process of development from an embryo to a baby or even to an adult then no line can be drawn anywhere in the process and whatever moral standing is assigned to babies or adults must be given to embryos. This position, although argued with great fervour by proponents of embryonic equality, makes little sense metaphysically or ethically.

We certainly do draw important distinctions both in kind and moral status between what a minor child can do and is responsible for and what an adult can do and the acts for which they are responsible. It may be hard to decide whether a man is bald but there are plainly bald men and hairy men. Arguing that an entity which may have the potential to become something else if conditions are exactly right is to falsely equate acorns with oak trees both as things and as objects of moral value. Someone who has plaque in their arteries may be a heart attack waiting to happen, but as the purveyors and consumers of statins and stents know it is far better to be a potential heart attack than an actual one.

Those who hold that consensus cannot be reached by rational argument and debate over the most contentious bioethical issues need to take notice of what is happening in the embryo wars. Although there are significant numbers of people who remain persuaded that the embryo must be treated as a person with full dignity and rights and others who still are not certain, this does not mean that huge areas of consensus concerning the creation and use of embryos in therapy and research have not been attained. And they have been attained through the entry into the debate of scientists offering facts about embryos, as well as by ethicists engaging claims of moral equality and refuting or at least casting doubt upon them. Bioethical debate may be acrimonious, opaque, religious, politically charged, and even personal but when science and logic are engaged it can lead to crucially important points of consensus.

> *"Pluripotent stem cells [are] an answer to prayer of pro-life advocates who have long desired an ethical medical solution to combat debilitating diseases and illnesses."*

Induced Pluripotent Stem Cell Research Is More Ethical than Embryonic Stem Cell Research

Andy Lewis

Andy Lewis is a research editor for the Ethics & Religious Liberty Commission, an entity of the Southern Baptist Convention that is dedicated to addressing social and moral concerns and their implications on public policy issues. In the following viewpoint, Lewis contends that induced pluripotent stem (iPS) cell research is ethically superior to embryonic stem cell research. According to Lewis, because iPS cells are pluripotent and are created from adult stem cells they do not have the ethical dilemmas associated with embryonic stem cell research. This is a win for pro-life Christians says Lewis, because iPS cells can cure diseases without embryo destruction.

As you read, consider the following questions:

1. According to Lewis, when it comes to forming cells, what is the difference between multipotent and pluripotent stem cells?

2. According to the author, what kind of adult cells did researchers from Japan and Wisconsin use to create induced pluripotent stem cells in November 2007?

3. According to Lewis, Christians should not be content with the identification of a process to create pluripotent stem cells from adult cells but should continue to do what?

In the past few months [in late 2007], three research teams have published reports outlining their successes in transforming adult skin cells into pluripotent stem cells, the functional equivalent of embryonic stem cells. These biotechnological breakthroughs have the potential to make a significant and positive impact on the state of the stem cell debate in America, as it could end the ethical dilemma regarding embryonic stem cells. With the present successes of several multipotent, non-embryonic stem cells in combating illness and the recent achievements of transforming skin cells into pluripotent stem cells, it is now time to end the debate about using embryonic stem cells. Stem cell funding should be targeted toward proven techniques (non-embryonic stem cells such as umbilical cord blood, placentas, and fat and bone marrow) and those techniques without ethical dilemmas (the new skin cell transformation techniques).

Pluripotency from an Adult Stem Cell

Stem cells are routinely classified into two categories, multipotent stem cells and pluripotent stem cells. Multipotent stem cells have the ability to form many of the body's cell types, but not all of them. Pluripotent stem cells, however, have the ability to develop into all types of the body's cells. Because of this unique flexibility, pluripotent stem cells have been the target of researchers and many in the scientific community, but, until now, pluripotent stem cells have had a serious ethical drawback—they were only able to be harvested from human embryos, which resulted in the destruction of human life. This has led many Christian groups and others concerned about the sanctity of human life to oppose this type of research in favor of the limited but morally positive alternative of multipotent stem cells. Yet, recent discoveries of induced pluripotent stem cells from adult skin cells provide the opportunity to realize the possible medical breakthroughs that pluripotent stem cells are capable of without having to be concerned about destroying nascent human life.

In November 2007 a research group in Japan and another in Wisconsin published results in *Cell* of scientific processes which successfully reprogrammed skin cells into stem cells that have functionally similar properties of embryonic stem cells, primarily that they are pluripotent and can develop into any cell type in the human body. These cells, when injected into mice, formed heart, muscle, and bone tissue. However, these results published in the *Cell* article identified one potential problem: the reprogrammed stem cells had a tendency to transform into cancerous cells. This problem appears to have been short-lived, though, because on November 30, 2007 Shinya Yamanaka of Kyoto University, the leader of the Japanese research groups, published results in *Nature Biotechnology* declaring that he was able to reproduce the stem cell creation process and eliminate the cancerous tendency by eliminating one of the four genes originally used. In the first process, six of the thirty-six mice injected with the cells died of tumors within 100 days, but in the second process, no mice died.

In a December 23, 2007 article in *Nature*, scientists at Harvard Medical School and Children's Hospital in Boston also

Respectable Science

Many Americans consider research on human embryos to be fundamentally wrong. Even some who do not share this conviction are nonetheless uneasy with using human embryos as research material. [Embryonic stem cell pioneer] James Thomson recently remarked in an interview with the *New York Times*, "If human embryonic stem cell research does not make you at least a little bit uncomfortable, you have not thought about it enough." *Good* research, research that truly advances our knowledge, enhances our lives, and ennobles our culture, must respect both scientific and ethical standards. [Induced pluripotent stem cell] research meets the highest standards of science, and it respects the ethical standards of many Americans who object to human embryonic stem cell research as deeply immoral.

Maureen Condic, First Things, *February 2008.*

reported that they were able to transform skin cells into the functional equivalent of embryonic stem cells. Unlike the research done in Japan and Wisconsin, the research at Harvard was conducted from natural skin cells from a human volunteer, not skin cells grown in a lab, providing further evidence that there is great promise in the skin cell reprogramming process.

Curing Diseases Without Ethical Dilemmas

Induced pluripotent stem cells, such as the stem cells created by these three research groups, provide an outstanding opportunity for modern science. While the positive results of this process are in the early stages of research, it appears to be feasible to achieve the positive results of pluripotent stem cells without destroying human life. This process, if continued to be proven successful, would be a clear victory for science, human life, and Christian advocacy. This process should eliminate embryonic stem cell research in favor of a functionally equivalent process without the ethical dilemmas. This result would allow pro-life Christians to hold both the moral and scientific high ground, as inducing pluripotent stem cells should provide all the advantages of embryonic stem cells without destroying human life.

The breakthrough of inducing skin cells into pluripotent stem cells is an answer to prayer of pro-life advocates, who have long desired an ethical medical solution to combat debilitating diseases and illnesses in society. However, Christians cannot be content with the mere success of identifying a process to create pluripotent stem cells from non-embryonic processes. Many in the scientific and political communities will undoubtedly continue to argue that embryonic stem cell research should continue until there is further evidence of the success of induced pluripotent stem cells and because there has already been much time, effort, and capital invested in the embryonic stem cell process. Thus, Christians should continue to stand up for innocent life, taking a strong stand against all forms of embryo-destructive stem cell research.

Human life is an amazing gift from God, and, as His creation, we must respect and honor this gift by seeking to protect innocent life, being good stewards of this gift, and operating in humble submission to the Creator. Therefore, Christians should continue to oppose all forms of embryo-destructive stem cell research, support current non-embryonic stem cell research, and begin advocating for more resources to be allocated to the research of induced pluripotent stem cells. The war against embryo-destructive stem cell research has not concluded with these recent discoveries, but they provide great hope for a scientific solution that provides both protection of innocent life and life-saving medical technologies.

| "*[Induced pluripotent stem] cell research involves challenging moral and legal issues.*"

Induced Pluripotent Stem Cells Present Ethical Concerns

Matthew Hoberg

Matthew Hoberg is a doctoral student in philosophy at the University of California, Berkeley. In the following viewpoint, Hoberg cautions opponents of embryonic stem cell research from celebrating the morality of induced pluripotent stem (iPS) cell research. According to Hoberg, there are grave moral concerns associated with the ability to use iPS cells to create human sperm and egg cells. Creation of these reproductive cells from skin cells or other somatic (i.e., nonreproductive) cells will enable the creation of human embryos through asexual reproduction, which Hoberg says is "intrinsically immoral." He calls for new laws to prohibit such reproduction.

As you read, consider the following questions:

1. What does Hoberg say researchers at the Harvard Stem Cell Institute used instead of viruses to transform skin cells into induced pluripotent stem cells?

2. Which states does the author say have laws against therapeutic cloning?

3. According to Hoberg, what will be more important than ever once the raw material for someone to be a parent can be provided by their tissue?

Scientists have recently developed a safe and efficient method to create induced pluripotent stem (iPS) cells from adult skin cells. Many opponents of embryonic stem cell research hail this news as an important step away from research methods that rely on destroying embryos. Despite this advance, the future of iPS cell research involves challenging moral and legal issues.

The Future Is Now

The therapeutic promise of stem cell research rests on using pluripotent stem cells, which can be grown into many of the types of cells found in the human body. Until recently, such cells could be produced only by destroying human embryos and harvesting embryonic stem cells. Opponents of embryonic stem cell research (ESCR) sought a method of producing pluripotent cells without destroying embryos. Their goal was to show that adult cells, rather than embryos, could provide the raw material for stem-cell therapy.

In 2007, scientists demonstrated that they could transform human skin cells into iPS cells, bypassing the destruction of embryos. While opponents of ESCR hailed this announcement as a sign that iPS cells could provide the full therapeutic promise of ES cells, the methods were still in their infancy. It took about a month for the iPS cells to develop, and very few transformations were successful: 99.9% of treated cells failed to transform. Besides being slow and unreliable, the techniques were dangerous. Viruses were used to insert specific genes into the adult cells, which increased the cancer risk for the stem cells and thus for prospective patients receiving stem cell therapy. Without a safer technique, the promise of iPS cell research remained in the future.

That future is now. On September 30 [2010] researchers led by Derrick J. Rossi, Ph.D., at the Harvard Stem Cell Institute reported a novel technique for producing iPS cells from adult skin cells that is fast, reliable, and safe. Instead of viruses, Rossi's team transformed skin cells using messenger RNA (mRNA), producing iPS cells two times faster and one hundred times more reliably than the virus techniques. Most importantly, the mRNA method does not raise the cancer risk for the iPS cells. While there is still room for improvement in the method's efficiency, scientists in the field view Rossi's discovery as a major breakthrough. Robert Lanza, chief scientific officer at Advanced Cell Technology, likens it to "turning lead into gold."

Embryonic Stem Cell Research Obsolete

Opponents of ESCR have applauded the discovery as well, citing its potential to render obsolete research methods that destroy embryos. Richard Doerflinger, Deputy Director of the Secretariat for Pro-Life Activities at the United States Conference of Catholic Bishops, commented: "With each new study it becomes more and more implausible to claim that scientists must rely on destruction of human embryos to achieve rapid progress in regenerative medicine."

With the new mRNA method for producing iPS cells the prospects for iPS cell research are better than ever. In this respect opponents of ESCR should welcome the news. They should be aware, however, that it is no moral panacea.

To begin with, demand for embryonic stem cells will continue in the near future. In order to determine that the transformations work properly and the cells are safe for therapeutic use, researchers need to compare the iPS cells to ES cells, which means destroying embryos. In the long run, fewer em-

Unjustifiable Enthusiasm

In fact, the enthusiasm with which hES [human embryonic stem] cell opponents greeted iPS [induced pluripotent stem] cell technology is not yet entirely justifiable—either in scientific or ethical terms. . . .

Nor is it clear that this technology really solves the ethical problem of embryo destruction that has generated the opposition to hES cell research. iPS cell technology brings an adult cell back to its pluripotent embryonic state. As the work of [Andras] Nagy and others has shown, with appropriate technical manipulations and sufficient support, such a cell might have the potential to develop into a human being. Since opponents of stem cell research and therapeutic cloning research usually base their arguments for the sanctity of fertilised or nuclear transfer embryos on precisely this kind of developmental capacity, it is not clear why they have not voiced similar concerns about iPS cell technology.

R.M. Green, Journal of Medical Ethics, *2008.*

bryos may be destroyed in stem-cell research as research shifts to iPS cells; but this transition may take years.

Moral Complications

The moral complications of the new state of the art go even deeper, due to an advance that scientists anticipate within a decade: using iPS cells to create human sperm and egg cells. Scientists will be able to create an entire embryo using ordinary skin cells or other adult cells, without *ever* using gametes [egg or sperm cells] harvested from a person. This method, which we might call *gameteless reproduction*, makes in vitro fertilization look like child's play and gives us more control than ever over human reproduction. The prospect of gamete-less reproduction not only makes even more pressing the on-going debate about the morality and legality of human clon-ing, but also raises moral and legal questions that are not widely known and discussed, even among the staunchest op-ponents of ESCR.

First, there are the moral issues connected with the proce-dure itself. Like Somatic Cell Nuclear Transfer (SCNT), the method used to clone Dolly [the sheep] in 1996, gameteless reproduction raises the question of the morality of cloning and other kinds of asexual reproduction, since it allows the creation of an embryo from one or more tissue donors. How-ever, gameteless reproduction has the potential to transform reproduction even more dramatically than SCNT. Unlike SCNT, gameteless reproduction uses easily obtainable adult tissue and does not require donated ova, which can be ob-tained only through a highly invasive procedure. It will thus be a dramatically cheaper and easier route to asexual repro-duction, and may therefore be much more widely used than SCNT. Due to its advantage over SCNT, gameteless reproduc-tion may over time replace IVF as the assisted reproductive technology of choice. Since it allows reproduction without do-nated sperm or eggs, gameteless reproduction expands the possibilities of reproduction. In principle, young children or deceased persons could become parents of embryos used in research. Moreover, gameteless reproduction may erode the link between procreation and any kind of family context: single persons, for example, could create an embryo using only their genetic material. As a result, children could be in-creasingly—and tragically—viewed as products, rather than the fruit of a loving relationship. Most importantly, like other non-conjugal methods of conception that sever the procre-ative and unitive aspects of human sexuality, gameteless re-production is intrinsically immoral.

Despite the anticipated development of gameteless reproduction and the serious moral questions it raises, this technique (like SCNT) is permitted under federal law. Only six states (Arkansas, Indiana, Iowa, Michigan, North Dakota, and South Dakota) have laws against therapeutic cloning, but only the Indiana law is broad enough to cover gameteless reproduction. We should expand existing prohibitions on cloning to cover gameteless reproduction as well.

Apart from these issues with the procedure itself, gameteless reproduction will also give parents an extraordinary level of control over the genetic makeup of their children. What moral principles govern these choices? Are parents morally required to create the "best" possible children? And should the law prevent parents from choosing to create children with disabilities?

Protecting Reproduction

Every human life is worth living, even a life beset by extraordinary hardship or disability. This is the foundation for protecting all human life, including the very young, the very old, and the physically and mentally disabled. It is therefore never wrong, in and of itself, to choose to bring a new human life into existence, though it may be wrong to do so with certain intentions, in certain circumstances, and through certain means. As I said earlier, non-conjugal reproduction is intrinsically immoral, and this is so because it involves an impermissible means of conception. In itself, however, choosing to conceive a child is a fundamentally good act. I therefore reject the view held by Joseph Spoerl (Professor of Philosophy at St. Anselm College), who has argued that choosing to conceive a child is to treat the future child as a means to the parents' ends, since the child does not yet exist and therefore cannot be benefitted by the choice. On the contrary, in choosing to conceive, parents are taking the necessary first steps for their child to come into existence; provided they are not making these choices for selfish reasons, they are not treating their child as a means only and are acting permissibly. This is a delicate issue, and I firmly agree with Ryan T. Anderson that we need to devote more attention to the intrinsic moral status of reproduction.

In recognition of the goodness of conception in itself, we should protect the choices of parents to have children who share their disabilities. If deaf parents foresee that conceiving a child through a conjugal act would result in a congenitally deaf child, that choice is morally permissible and should be legally protected. It does *not* follow that deliberately choosing a deaf child through embryonic selection is permissible.

There's another argument in favor of protecting the reproductive choices of the disabled. The law not only governs our behavior but also expresses our values. Prohibiting parents from knowingly conceiving a severely disabled child, on the grounds that their doing so would lead the child to have a life not worth living, expresses profound disrespect for the value of each human life. Importantly, even if it's controversial that every life is worth living, it's arguable that the law should pro- ceed as though it were true because not doing so would dishonor those who live with disabilities. How can society claim to value the deaf, or those with other disabilities, if it requires that their children not resemble them in these respects?

Tissue Donation

Though it is seldom discussed among opponents of ESCR, there is a further set of issues that gameteless reproduction raises: how should we regulate tissue donation in light of future advances in reproductive technology? Donating tissue for scientific research will soon mean donating tissue that can be used to grow a sperm or egg; tissue donors could then become parents at the whim of the researchers possessing their tissue. While it has always been important for tissue donors to have some control over what procedures are done with their samples—some donors might be comfortable with certain kinds of research, and others might not—informed consent will be more important than ever once a simple cheek swab provides the raw material for someone to be a mother or father. There is disagreement in the courts and legal academy about whether there is a constitutional right not to be a parent; there should be no dispute that it is gravely immoral to make someone a parent (even of the most nascent form of human life, the embryo) without their informed consent.

The current law governing informed consent for tissue donation is woefully inadequate for protecting tissue donors in light of anticipated progress with iPS cell research. Informed consent is required when donating tissue for therapeutic research, in which the patient stands to benefit from the treatment being tested; violating the informed consent requirement is a tort. However, when donors give tissue to nontherapeutic research, in which they will not benefit from experimental treatment, violating informed consent is punished through administrative measures, like denial of federal funding. This minor response is clearly inadequate for the moral gravity of using someone's tissue to make them a parent without their consent.

Moreover, once the tissue has been donated, there is no further risk of harm to the donor. This means that there is no legal informed consent requirement whenever obtaining a consent waiver is impractical and the tissue can no longer be linked back to the donor. If these two conditions are met, which is not uncommon, there are no restrictions related to informed consent for how researchers can use a donor's tissue. In the absence of a sufficiently wide ban on human cloning and gameteless reproduction, or a legally protected right not to be a parent, researchers in these scenarios have a legal green light to make tissue donors parents without any kind of consent; this is profoundly immoral and should be a legally actionable tort.

Harnessing Scientific Momentum

As new advances alter the possibilities of human reproduction, we must develop a morally sound body of law governing stem cell research and tissue donation. Science studies momentum and other physical quantities but it also has its own momentum, which we must harness to promote the common good.

> "To pursue [stem cell] research is a moral choice. Not to pursue it is a moral choice. And moral choices of this nature properly wind up in the political arena."

The Morality of Stem Cell Research Is Linked to Politics

Peter Steinfels

Peter Steinfels is an American journalist, educator, and the author of several books, such as The Neoconservatives: The Men Who Are Changing America's Politics *and* A People Adrift: The Crisis of the Roman Catholic Church in America. *In the following viewpoint, Steinfels asserts that the morality of stem cell research should be decided in the political arena. According to Steinfels, many people think that scientific questions—such as whether to pursue human embryonic stem cell research—should be answered without political influence. However, Steinfels believes that whether or not to pursue human embryonic stem cell research is really a moral question, which is appropriately decided within the scope of politics.*

As you read, consider the following questions:

1. According to Steinfels, what former president's son told an audience to imagine "your own personal biological repair kit standing by at the hospital?"

2. According to the author, historians, sociologists, and scientists have generated a small library of books demonstrating what?

3. According to Steinfels, two days after President Obama's announcement lifting restrictions on federally funded human embryonic stem cell research, the *New York Times* ran a page 1 article about European nations debating what?

Almost no one was surprised this week [March 14, 2009,] when President [Barack] Obama lifted restrictions on stem cell research that involved the destruction of human embryos. Even jaded Washington watchers are adjusting to the idea that this is a president with an eerie determination to do exactly what he said he would do during his campaign.

Those who approve such research applauded Mr. Obama's action. ("Fantastic," said one stem cell scientist on PBS.) Those who disapprove condemned it. ("Deadly," said an anti-abortion leader in *The New York Times*.) But some commentary focused at least as much on the nature of the president's moral argument as on the specific conclusions he reached.

A Missing Moral Argument

When it comes to the controversy over human embryonic stem cell research, moral argument has not been much in evidence. The president spoke of a popular consensus in favor of it reached "after much discussion, debate and reflection." That is a kindly description of the hype, exaggeration and denunciation that have dominated the controversy.

Politicians, scientists and Hollywood stars conjured up visions of cures of biblical proportions. One member of the House of Representatives equated opposition to embryonic stem cell research with refusing "a cure for your child's cancer." Another called such opposition "a sentence of death of millions of Americans."

Not long after the death of former President Ronald Reagan, his younger son, Ron, told delegates at the 2004 Democratic convention to imagine "your own personal biological repair kit standing by at the hospital."

"Sound like magic?" Mr. Reagan said. "Welcome to the future of medicine."

Scientists who knew better kept quiet.

"People need a fairy tale," Ronald D.G. McKay, a stem cell researcher at the National Institute of Neurological Disorders and Stroke, explained to *The Washington Post* in 2004.

Recently, Nicholas Wade in the Science section of *The New York Times* summed this all up: "Members of Congress and advocates for fighting diseases have long spoken of human embryonic stem cell research as if it were a sure avenue to quick cures for intractable afflictions. Scientists have not publicly objected to such high-flown hopes, which have helped fuel new sources of grant money like the $3 billion initiative in California for stem cell research."

"In private, however," the article continued, "many researchers have projected much more modest goals for embryonic stem cells."

Mr. Obama certainly avoided the worst of this recent history. He warned twice against overstating the promise of stem cell research, even if he did envision "a day when words like 'terminal' and 'incurable' are finally retired from our vocabulary."

More important, he acknowledged that "thoughtful and decent people" opposed this research, and he claimed to "understand their concerns." His own view was that "with proper guidelines and strict oversight, the perils can be avoided."

What were those "concerns" that Mr. Obama understood or those "perils" that he would avoid? The president did not say. So one could object that his moral argument stopped in mid-air. How can one evaluate what he called "a difficult and delicate balance" when it is not clear exactly what is being balanced?

The more challenging objection—again, not to the president's specific stance on embryonic stem cell research, but to the general form of his argument—went directly to a theme running through his announcement and echoed in enthusiastic comments from research proponents:

Science, it was said, should be isolated from politics, from ideology, from dogma, from religion.

Science, Morality, and Politics

Sounds good if all one means is that the current administration will treat science with more respect than many people believe its predecessor did. Sounds good if all one means by politics is partisan maneuvering or by ideology, dogma and religion, some form of blind belief unwilling to engage alternative viewpoints.

But these words frequently function as weapons. One person's ideology can be someone else's political philosophy or even morality. One person's dogma can be someone else's self-evident truths. And politics is the way that people decide how they will live together, by what moral standards and to what ends.

Historians, sociologists and scientists themselves have generated a small library of books demonstrating how much of science has been driven and shaped by politics and ideology—and economics, too—all the while imagining that it was value-free, "just the facts," as Sergeant Friday [of the 1960s TV police drama *Dragnet*] and perhaps Mr. Obama would say.

Science has certainly developed safeguards to isolate its work from distorting influences. The danger is that those safeguards, like antibodies run amok, can also isolate it from morality.

In a provocative article in online magazine *Slate*, William Saletan, a supporter of embryonic stem cell research, noted the "mirror image" of some research advocacy by pointing to [former aide to George W. Bush] Karl Rove's accusation that Mr. Obama was endangering the country by drawing a sharp moral line against certain methods of interrogation.

"Proponents of embryo research are insisting that because we're in a life-and-death struggle—in this case, a scientific struggle—anyone who impedes that struggle by renouncing effective tools is irrational and irresponsible," Mr. Saletan wrote. "The war on disease is like the war on terror. Either you're with science or you're against it."

To label the opposition to embryonic stem cell research as "ideology," Mr. Saletan suggests, is to "forget the moral problem." To pursue this research is a moral choice. Not to pursue it is a moral choice. And moral choices of this nature properly wind up in the political arena.

Two days after Mr. Obama's announcement, the *Times* ran three science-related articles. One was about stem cell researchers worried that any new federal financing might prove insufficient. It also ran an article about a prolific medical researcher who admitted fabricating research that just happened to support the products of the pharmaceutical company underwriting the research. Both were reminders of how much science is affected by big money.

And the paper ran a Page 1 article about European nations' debating whether surgical or chemical castration is an effective, humane and legitimate treatment to rehabilitate violent sex offenders. No one can read that article and imagine that this is simply a scientific question, to be resolved by medical scientists on their own terms, rather than one that is profoundly moral and political.

Is that any less true when it comes to not only human embryonic stem cell research but also a host of other ethically fraught, knotty scientific questions now challenging Americans?

Periodical and Internet Sources Bibliography

The following articles have been selected to supplement the diverse views presented in this chapter.

Catholic News Service	"Catholic Couple Blazes New Trails in Adult Cardiac Stem-Cell Research," May 3, 2011.
Sherif Girgis	"Stem Cells: The Scientists Knew They Were Lying?," *Public Discourse*, April 13, 2011.
Adam Keiper and Yuval Levin	"Stem Cells, Life, and the Law," *Human Life Review*, Summer 2010.
Louis Klostergaard	"Embryonic Stem Cell Research Is Not Dehumanizing Us," *Journal of Medical Ethics*, December 2009.
M. William Lensch and Mahendra Rao	"Induced Pluripotent Stem Cells: Opportunities and Challenges," *Regenerative Medicine*, July 2010.
Jeanne Loring	"Cell Fate," *Technology Review*, July/August 2009.
Karen Perry	"The New Biology," *Library Media Connection*, March/April 2011.
Sally Quinn, Jon Meacham, and On Faith Panelists	"The (Im)Morality of Stem Cell Research," *Washington Post*, March 6–16, 2009.
Wesley J. Smith	"Pulling the Plug on the Conscience Clause," *First Things*, December 2009.
Patrick Tucker	"Abortion, Stem Cells, and How Morality Works: Reinventing Morality, Part 2: An Interview with Marc Hauser," *Encyclopedia Britannica Blog*, January 14, 2009.

CHAPTER 3

What Kind of Embryos Should Be Used for Embryonic Stem Cell Research?

Chapter Preface

Abortion is among the most contentious issues in US history. In 1973, when the United States Supreme Court ruled in the landmark case of *Roe v. Wade* that a woman has a legal right to terminate her pregnancy, it generated a culture war pitting pro-life, or antiabortion advocates, against those who believe abortion is a woman's right, or pro-choice advocates. Soon after *Roe v. Wade* was decided, state legislatures around the country began enacting laws to restrict abortions and protect human embryos and fetuses. Many of these 1970s state abortion laws have had important impacts on scientists' ability to perform human embryonic stem cell research. As debates about abortion and human embryonic stem cell research have continued into the twenty-first century, some states have considered enacting laws maintaining that fertilized human eggs, or embryos, are "persons" under the law. These laws could prohibit abortion and the creation of new human embryonic stem cell lines.

The organization Personhood USA has been at the forefront of the movement to get embryos classified as persons under state laws. Personhood USA was formed in Colorado in 2008 by two pro-life advocates, Keith Mason and Cal Zastrow. In 2008, Mason and Zastrow were able to get a proposition put before Colorado voters that would have amended the state's constitution to define the term *person* to include any human being from the moment of conception. Adopting such a constitutional amendment would have provided fertilized human egg cells or embryos with inalienable rights, equality of justice, and due process under the law, thus potentially banning abortion and human embryonic stem cell research. Colorado voters soundly defeated the amendment. However, Personhood USA got the amendment back on the ballot in subsequent years and started a nationwide movement to enact personhood laws in more than thirty other states. Daniel Becker, president of Georgia Right to Life, explained the importance of personhood laws in his 2011 book *Personhood: A Pragmatic Guide to Prolife Victory in the 21st Century and the Return to First Principles in Politics.* "Abortion, euthanasia, destructive stem cell research, human-animal hybrids and cloning—the question of 'Personhood' is at the center of every one of these assaults on human life and dignity," wrote Becker.

Pro-choice organizations, women's rights groups, and secular groups are opposed to personhood laws. They argue that personhood laws would elevate the rights of embryos above those of pregnant women. The organization, National Advocates for Pregnant Women (NAPW), contends that pregnant women would lose all their civil and human rights and privacy protections if personhood laws were enacted. Women who have miscarriages or stillbirths could be prosecuted for murder, manslaughter, or negligent homicide, says the organization. Additionally, according to the NAPW, doctors in many states could be forced to report women who do not take their prenatal vitamins or who drink a glass of wine while pregnant. In a March 2009 editorial, Lynn Paltrow, founder and executive director of NAPW, wrote, "Personhood USA asserts that 'each and every human being must be respected and protected from fertilization until natural death.' Their legislation, however, would have the effect of excluding pregnant women from this protection. People committed to a true culture of life need to oppose their legislative proposals, supporting instead ones that include the interests of the women who give that life."

The Coalition for Secular Government (CSG) calls personhood laws "anti-life." According to the CSG, personhood laws hurt more than just pregnant women. The organization argues that these laws would ban all medical research that might harm embryos—even though such research may help save and improve the lives of countless "born people." In a CSG policy paper published on August 31, 2010, Ari Armstrong and Diana Hsieh, wrote "in the name of respecting life, personhood advocates would impose a death sentence on the real people whose lives might be saved through embryonic stem cell research."

How individuals and groups answer the question of when life begins generally shapes their view on many bioethical issues. The contributors to the following chapter provide their viewpoints on the ethical issues surrounding the use of different kinds of embryos in stem cell research.

"Isn't it worse to discard an embryo than to use the embryo for research and development of treatments for currently incurable diseases?"

Excess IVF Embryos Should Be Used for Stem Cell Research

Maude Rowland and Kirstin Matthews

Maude Rowland is a graduate intern and Kirstin Matthews a fellow in science and technology policy at the James A. Baker III Institute for Public Policy at Rice University in Houston, Texas. In the following viewpoint, Rowland and Matthews maintain that frozen embryos remaining after the completion of a successful in vitro fertilization (IVF) procedure should be used as a source of stem cells. According to Rowland and Matthews, using excess IVF embryos for research is morally equivalent to their current fate, being thawed and discarded. Given the help that embryonic stem cell research can someday provide to people who are suffering from debilitating diseases, Rowland and Matthews question why there is such controversy over using excess IVF embryos for research.

As you read, consider the following questions:

1. Who won the 2010 Nobel Prize in physiology or medicine for the development of in vitro fertilization (IVF), as cited by the authors?

2. According to Rowland and Matthews, what is the US equivalent of the UK's Medical Research Council?

3. What do the authors say is one of the National Institutes of Health's requirements for the use of human embryonic stem cell lines in federally funded experiments?

This week [October 7, 2010,] the Nobel Prize in physiology [or] medicine was awarded to British scientist Robert Edwards, Ph.D., for the development of in vitro fertilization (IVF). Edwards, along with his colleague Patrick Steptoe, M.D., who died in 1988, perfected this laboratory technique, which allows infertile couples to have children. Since the birth of Louise Brown in 1978 in the United Kingdom, the first baby born as a result of IVF, millions of people have used the procedure to have children.

When IVF was first deemed possible, many in the U.K. feared that it would result in "test tube babies," and the U.K.'s Medical Research Council, the U.K.'s equivalent to the U.S. National Institutes of Health (NIH), refused to fund the research. Now many groups who once opposed IVF—and a majority of the public—generally accept the procedure's use as a treatment for infertility.

IVF's Excess Embryos

IVF involves the removal of eggs from a woman. The eggs are then fertilized with the father's sperm in a laboratory, and implanted back into the mother. During the IVF process several embryos are created, but typically only a few are implanted to avoid a multiple pregnancy (such as quadruplets), which is extremely dangerous to the mother and babies. The remaining embryos are frozen, and the couple later decides what it wants to do with them. Some of the embryos are used by the couple, some are adopted by other couples and some are donated to science. However, many of the embryos are thawed and discarded, particularly after several years in storage. These discarded embryos do not seem to be as controversial to the public as the human embryonic stem cell lines that could be created from embryos donated to research.

The timing of the Nobel Prize is particularly interesting due to the court case *Sherley v. Sibelius*, currently being ruled on in U.S. District Court. As discussed in the Aug. 31 [2010] Baker Institute blog post, "Stem cell ruling hurts Texas scientists too," this case is determining if federal funding can be used for human embryonic stem cell research.

Currently, the NIH must approve all human embryonic stem cell lines before they can be used in federally funded experiments. (The NIH does not fund the actual creation of human embryonic stem cell lines.) One of the requirements is that the lines must be created from discarded IVF embryos with proper informed consent. These embryos are already in existence; they were not created for research purposes but for reproductive purposes.

Puzzling Controversy

With such wide support for IVF, it is remarkable that there is still such a public outcry in the United States over the use of leftover embryos for scientific research. From a moral standpoint, one can argue that in both cases an embryo is destroyed and the destruction of an embryo is always wrong. But isn't it worse to discard an embryo than to use the embryo for research and development of treatments for currently incurable diseases? Embryonic stem cell research has the po-

Complex Attitudes Toward Embryos

Plenty of people in our society care about the fate of frozen embryos, from scientists who see potential in stem-cell and other kinds of research to members of religious groups who consider embryos to be full human beings with rights that need to be protected. In the political arena, the fight often assumes that infertility patients will have—or can be persuaded to have—one of two diametric views: An embryo is a life, or an embryo isn't a life. But patients themselves express far more complex attitudes toward these tiny clusters of cells and may experience an emotional attachment that, though heartfelt, doesn't always correspond with viewing embryos as children-in-waiting.

Alison Lobron,
Boston Globe, *November 22, 2009.*

tential to bring relief to people suffering from diseases such as Parkinson's disease, muscular dystrophy and diabetes, as well as catastrophic injuries including those to the spinal cord.

It should be unnecessary to create embryos for research purposes with the number of existing IVF embryos not being used. These embryos can provide scientists with human embryonic stem cell lines to develop cures for devastating diseases, as long as research using these lines can be federally funded.

Perhaps in 30 years, we will look back puzzled as to why the use of human embryonic stem cells was so controversial, given the extensive contributions this type of research will have made to therapies for debilitating diseases. And, when the pioneers of stem cell research win a Nobel Prize, the American public will be excited—and appreciative.

| "Embryos should never be sacrificed
upon the altar of biomedical research."

Excess IVF Embryos Should Not Be Used for Research

Thomas Berg

Thomas Berg is a Catholic priest and the director of the Westchester Institute for Ethics and the Human Person, a research institute conducting interdisciplinary, natural law analysis of complex, contemporary moral issues. In the following viewpoint, Berg asserts that it is never acceptable to kill an embryo for the purpose of biomedical research. Berg blames the entire in vitro fertilization (IVF) industry for the moral predicament of what to do with surplus embryos. He suggests that none of the options available to couples with leftover embryos is very good, but he believes the worst and most immoral option is to kill the embryos for research.

As you read, consider the following questions:

1. How many embryos were estimated to be preserved in liquid nitrogen at US IVF clinics, according to a 2003 report by the Rand Corporation cited by the author?

2. According to Berg, what are the options that couples with surplus IVF embryos are forced to choose from?

3. The author says he would not exclude the possibility of donating cells from an embryo under what circumstances?

A couple of weeks ago [September 10, 2007,] I wrote a column about StemLifeLine, a California company that has recently begun offering a unique service to couples who have created human embryos by means of in vitro fertilization (IVF). The company offers to take their remaining frozen (cryopreserved) embryos and "transform" them into "useful" stem cells. The company's entire premise—to take these embryos, destroy them, and derive from them stem cells that would be "customized" for use by either the father or mother—is, as I pointed out, a complete sham: tissues developed from stem cells derived from these embryos, if implanted in either parent, would require life-long immunosuppression, lest the tissues be rejected by their bodies. So much for "customized" stem cells. As I stated at the time, however, the very existence of this company—notwithstanding its phony advertising—is a powerful reminder that the age of embryo-based biomedicine is now upon us.

For the past two years, we have also seen significant efforts in the U.S. Congress to press for legislation that would "free up" the existing population of frozen IVF embryos for research purposes. In spite of these efforts, it is clear that under the present administration [of George W. Bush] the current federal prohibition on using federal funding to destroy IVF embryos for research will stand. (It may not in future administrations.)

IVF's Moral Dilemma

But such realities have brought to the forefront a difficult and disturbing moral question: what can be done ethically with those IVF embryos judged unsuitable or no longer intended for transfer into the womb?

In the survival-of-the-fittest world of IVF, multiple embryos are manufactured from the eggs and sperm of couples pursuing pregnancy by this means. Surplus embryos—those not implanted immediately—are placed in suspended animation, their initial cellular development arrested at the very outset of their existence, sometimes even at the one-cell stage. Immersed in a soup of cryoprotectant chemicals, then sucked into straws, these embryos are then entombed in tanks of liquid nitrogen and instantaneously frozen. Just under four hundred thousand such embryos are preserved in IVF clinics in the United States alone according to the most recent, reliable study produced in 2003 by the Rand Corporation.

The Catholic Church continues to teach that recourse to IVF as a remedy for infertility is morally illicit. The Church rejects this as a morally viable option on the grounds that children have a right to be brought into the world, not through the dexterity of lab technician's hand, but through the unitive and procreative act of conjugal intercourse of a man and woman united in marriage. Children brought into the world through IVF are not generated, but literally *manufactured*. While the Church endorses any number of licit means of *assisting* the marital act, we maintain that it is morally illicit to *substitute* that act with technical interventions—which is precisely what happens in the case of IVF.

What to Do with the Embryos?

There should not be 400,000+ human embryos currently stored in tanks of liquid nitrogen. The entire IVF enterprise is to be credited for bringing about this stunning and absurd moral predicament. The probing question that now faces so many IVF parents is: what to do with the remaining embryos that they do not intend to gestate?

Couples in this situation are forced to choose from the following options: allow their offspring to be kept in frozen storage indefinitely; have the embryos removed from frozen storage and allowed to expire naturally or be "disposed of" as laboratory waste; give up the embryos to scientific research; or give up the embryos for adoption by another couple.

I would suggest that choosing to keep the embryos in frozen storage indefinitely only delays the inevitable—eventual death through organismic decay while in the frozen state. Noting that the thawing process itself often kills IVF embryos being prepared for transfer, some moralists object to the prospect of a couple choosing to thaw their embryos, allowing them to expire naturally. I believe that a sound argument can be made for the removal of frozen embryos from their storage containers on the grounds that continued cryopreservation constitutes an extraordinary and ultimately futile means of continued existence—an absurd and tragic existence to be sure. Allowing the embryos to die is not the same as directly killing them. Directing lab technicians to "dispose" of the embryos is ethically unacceptable as this entails taking actions directly on the embryos with the intention of destroying them. A recent study conducted by the University of Pennsylvania discovered that protocols for the disposal of excess embryos at American IVF clinics vary in surprising ways, including quasi-religious ceremonies. The study also suggests that such disposal creates serious problems of conscience for clinicians, many of whom opt out of involvement in the disposal procedure.

Parents who decide to remove their embryos from frozen storage to allow them to die naturally should be encouraged to ask their pastor whether some blessing or other appropriate ceremony might be possible. The remaining embryos (though microscopic) should be treated with the degree of respect due to all human remains.

Obviously, embryos should never be sacrificed upon the altar of biomedical research. Such a decision would constitute a grave affront to human dignity and a direct assault on innocent human life. No putative medical benefit can justify the direct killing of a human being.

I would not exclude the possibility of donating cells from an embryo after its death. If a criterion for embryonic death can be established, it may be moral to donate cells from a deceased embryo just as one might from any child who dies.

Catholic theologians continue to be of diverse opinions, however, on the question of embryo adoption: the licitness, that is, of implanting unwanted IVF embryos into the wombs of women willing to gestate them to term with the intention of "rescuing" them from almost certain death, or even to adopt them outright. The Holy See [the Vatican] has not expressed a definitive moral judgment on the matter. Some theologians hold that such a proposition is not only morally licit, but even heroic. Others hold—at least in the case of married women—that such a prospect (which entails the woman's becoming pregnant apart from the intervention of her husband), though noble in its intention, would constitute a grave violation of the marriage covenant. . . .

A Moral Boundary

My on-going exposure to the field of embryonic stem cell (ESC) research compels me to believe that the interest in embryo-based scientific research is growing—research we should remember that might have little or nothing to do with eventual cures to which such research might directly or indirectly contribute. I am convinced that today we stand on the verge of an era in which such embryo-destructive research could become common-place. There are any number of grim indications that a majority of Americans are slowly being cajoled into endorsing such a barbarous plan. To avoid such a future, we must demand that lawmakers pursue a complete federal ban on the creation *in vitro* of human embryos for any purpose other than implantation in a human womb. Surely Americans have not yet reached such a state of moral confusion as to fail to see the reasonableness of such a moral boundary line. But I have reasons to wonder.

> "The anti-abortion forces who have de-
> layed stem-cell research by a decade
> are not morally serious. If they were,
> they would be trying to get laws mak-
> ing the work of fertility clinics illegal."

Truly Sincere Opponents of Embryonic Stem Cell Research Would Also Oppose IVF

Michael Kinsley

*Michael Kinsley is an American political journalist and televi-
sion commentator. He has worked for and contributed to many
publications and media outlets, including the* Daily Beast, Los
Angeles Times, Slate, Time, *and the* Washington Post. *In the
following viewpoint, Kinsley argues that those who say it is immoral to use embryos created by in vitro fertilization (IVF) for
research, but who accept the use of IVF to help infertile couples
have children are being insincere. According to Kinsley, IVF clinics produce thousands of embryos that go unused and are eventually discarded. If embryonic stem cell opponents were being
"morally serious," says Kinsley, they would oppose IVF procedures as passionately as they oppose the use of embryos for research.*

As you read, consider the following questions:

1. Which does Kinsley say has "no easy answers": a "quandary" or a "controversy"?

2. What does the author say the stem cell controversy is really about?

3. Why does Kinsley say that it makes a big difference whether embryonic stem cell research is stamped an "ethical quandary"?

You call this a quandary?

"Potentially closing the book on this decade's definitive medical ethical quandary," the *Daily Beast*'s Cheat Sheet reports (crediting the *Guardian*), "British and Canadian scientists have discovered a way to produce stem cells without destroying an embryo."

Quandry Versus Controversy

This is good news, to be sure. But let's be clear: There is NO "medical ethical quandary" involved in the decade-long dispute over stem cells. There is only the appearance of an ethical quandary, created by people who either don't understand or willfully misrepresent the facts. "Quandary" is a particularly insidious word. Compare it to "controversy." There is undeniably a controversy about stem cells: two sides, disagreeing strongly. But "quandary" suggests that the controversy is legitimate—that a fair-minded person would have to recognize some degree of merit in both sides of the argument, wherever he or she might ultimately come down. In a "quandary," there actually are (dread phrase) "no easy answers.". . .

The stem-cell controversy is really about abortion, of course. And abortion is both a controversy and, for most people, a genuine quandary. That quandary usually is defined as, "When does human life begin?" I think a better way to put it is, "When do human rights begin?" That avoids the whole hopeless search for agreement about some mystical moment when humanity is conferred, all of which (conception, birth, "quickening," sundry trimesters) are equally illogical, and concentrates on a question that can be debated or negotiated with some hope of progress. But many will disagree even with that preliminary assertion, claiming that it's a setup for the pro-choice answer I prefer. It's a quandary.

The debate over stem-cell research is different. There is a controversy, but no real quandary. Here is why. Virtually all stem cells used (or that will be used) in medical research come from fertility clinics. Standard operating procedure in fertility clinics is to fertilize and implant multiple eggs in the hope that at least one will survive. For that matter, Mother Nature's method of producing a human being is not very different in this regard, and also involves fertilizing far more eggs than ever grow into babies.

If you wish to believe that every fertilized egg is a human being with full human rights, that is your privilege. I disagree, which makes it a controversy. If I felt you were serious, we would have a quandary as well. But there's no quandary because you're not serious. Your actions are too different from your words. You are doing absolutely nothing about the millions of fertilized eggs that are destroyed naturally every year (in miscarriages so early that the potential mother is not even aware of them), or the thousands that are produced and unused by fertility clinics going about their normal work (which are either discarded or pointlessly frozen in the hope of some miraculous ethical breakthrough).

Opponents Are Insincere

The anti-abortion forces who have delayed stem-cell research by a decade are not morally serious. If they were, they would be trying to get laws making the work of fertility clinics illegal, not concentrating on the tiny fraction of surplus embryos

The "Disposition Decision"

A new demographic is wrestling with questions initially posed by contraception and abortion. A world away from the exigencies, mitigating circumstances, and carefully honed ideologies that have grown up in and around U.S. abortion clinics, it is people like Janis Elspas who are being called upon to think, hard, about when life begins, and when it is—or is not—right to terminate it. They are in this position, ironically enough, not because they don't want a family, but precisely because they do. Among the nation's growing ranks of IVF patients, deciding the fate of frozen embryos is known as the "disposition decision," and it is one of the hardest decisions patients face, so unexpectedly problematic that many decide, in the end, to punt, a choice that is only going to make the glut bigger, the moral problem more looming and unresolved.

Liza Mundy, Mother Jones, *July/August 2006.*

from those clinics that are going to a worthwhile purpose. They would still be severely mistaken, in my view, but at least that could legitimately be described as an "ethical quandary." But there is no political pressure against fertility clinics. While abortion clinics are routinely terrorized, fertility clinics advertise on the radio. If you really think that a microscopic embryo is a human being, which kind of clinic kills more human beings every year? It isn't even close.

What difference does this all make, now that George W. Bush is gone and his ban on federally funded stem-cell research has been eliminated? It makes a big difference. When something is stamped as an "ethical quandary," people and organizations that wish to avoid controversy stay away. Or they appoint well-meaning but slow-moving commissions to study the issue. Or they split the difference in some silly and irritating way. Whatever, the result is that the promise of stem-cell research is delayed or unrealized.

The essence of today's report is that scientists have found some incredibly complicated way to create—someday, maybe even soon—a valuable research tool that already exists by the thousands and has for years. Some people think we should have been using it for years, while others say they think using it would be immoral, but can't give a coherent reason. What a quandary.

> *"The attempt to apply one's principles pragmatically, and with an eye toward the art of the politically possible, isn't evidence that those principles don't exist."*

Opponents of Embryonic Stem Cell Research Can Be Truly Sincere and Still Compromise on IVF

Ross Douthat

Ross Douthat is a conservative columnist and blogger for the New York Times *and former editor of the* Atlantic. *In March 2009, Douthat and Michael Kinsley, author of the previous viewpoint, exchanged commentaries over the moral seriousness of embryonic stem cell research opponents. In the following viewpoint, Douthat objects to Kinsley's assertion that because embryonic stem cell opponents do not picket at in vitro fertilization (IVF) clinics, they are not morally sincere and do not mean what they say. According to Douthat, people in the pro-life movement have moral concerns about IVF; however, they have not been as vociferous in their objection to IVF as they have been to* embryonic stem cell research because they understand that the US political landscape requires them to compromise. The fact that pro-lifers are not trying to prohibit IVF does not mean that they have not thought about the moral connections between IVF and embryonic stem cell research, says Douthat, and it does not weaken their moral seriousness against the latter.

As you read, consider the following questions:

1. According to Douthat, some of the pro-life movement's bigger successes following *Roe v. Wade* have involved what?

2. What is the maximalist pro-life stance that the author says is already embedded in the GOP platform?

3. According to Douthat, some pro-lifers were prompted to seek to enact restrictions on fertility clinics because of public outrage over what?

Michael Kinsley was kind enough to respond to a post, in which I objected to his suggestion that pro-lifers who oppose embryo-destructive research don't mean what they say, because if they did they'd want to forbid embryo destruction in fertility clinics as well. He writes:

Douthat's reply was that (a) opponents of stem-cell research do indeed oppose the creation and destruction of all embryos in fertility clinics, and not just the ones that are used for scientific research; but (b) accepting fertility clinics as a given is a compromise with reality, and stem-cell opponents deserve congratulations for playing democracy according to the rules; and (c) in particular, they were, and are, simply asking not to be coerced through the tax system into having their dollars spent in a way they find morally repugnant.

Let's start with (c). Although it's rarely put this way, coercion—especially financial coercion—is at the heart of any political system, including democracy. Almost the whole point of politics is to decide what money is spent communally, and how. Obviously the system can't work if everyone gets to withhold tax dollars from projects they disapprove of. I and many others, for example, would have preferred to not to have our tax dollars go to finance the Iraq war. I'm sure Ross Douthat would have had no problem seeing why that wouldn't work.

No Zero-Sum Game

Well, sure. But policy choices aren't always a zero-sum game. In the case of the Iraq War, if the government didn't organize an invasion (using the anti-war minority's money to pay for it), it wasn't going to happen: Halliburton and the Blackwater Group weren't about to step up to the plate with a private-sector alternative. But embryonic stem cell research could happen in the absence of government involvement, and indeed it has—thanks to my own alma mater [Harvard], among other institutions.

This doesn't make a half-a-loaf compromise, in which the research is allowed but left unfunded, something that Michael Kinsley has to accept. He has every right to seek the coercion of his pro-life antagonists and the use of their tax dollars for the research that he favors; such coercion, as he says, is a normal feature of democratic life. But the fact that he prefers to seek the full loaf doesn't mean that a compromise isn't possible, or that pro-lifers, conscious of the unfavorable landscape in which they're operating, shouldn't be agitating in its favor. After all, some of the pro-life movement's bigger successes, post-*Roe* [*v. Wade*, the 1973 Supreme Court decision that granted women the right to obtain legal abortions] have involved eliminating or reducing public funding for abortion, even as the procedure itself has remained legal and widely practiced. Fighting against government funding for stem-cell research is the equivalent of the Hyde Amendment [a legislative provision that prohibits federal funding of abortion] approach to government funding for abortion: It may not work, but that doesn't mean it doesn't make political sense.

Kinsley goes on:

If it was a tactical compromise to make an issue of stem-cell research while ignoring the vast majority of surplus embryos produced in fertility clinics that are simply destroyed, this compromise was a mighty strange one. Ordinarily, if you intend to compromise, you start by playing up your maximalist position as much as possible, emphasizing how strongly you feel and how difficult it will be to accept half a loaf. Then you compromise. In this case, though, Douthat can only point to a couple of columns by Will Saletan in *Slate*—one about the octuplets controversy [about the woman, dubbed "Octomom," who had multiple embryos implanted in an IVF procedure, eight of which went to term] and the other about some law in Italy—to support his contention that pro-lifers "would like to heavily regulate fertility clinics." Maybe they would, but this has played absolutely no part in the stem-cell debate. In [President George W.] Bush's original speech announcing his stem-cell research restrictions eight years ago (now praised by conservatives as a masterpiece of moral reasoning the way liberals praise President [Barack] Obama's speech on race in Philadelphia) Bush actually praised the work of fertility clinics, claiming—correctly—that in-vitro fertilization has brought happiness to many.

Actually, as [conservative columnist Daniel] Larison notes, Bush's speech came in for quite a bit of criticism from pro-lifers, many of whom eventually came around to defending it because it was clear from the political landscape that this was the best they could hope for. And is it *really* the case that with every new controversy and debate (and the stem-cell debate was very much a new one for pro-lifers in 2001), the thing to do is "play up your maximalist position as much as possible" before proposing compromises?

I think not. The maximalist pro-life stance—a Human Life Amendment to the U.S. Constitution, which would constrain fertility clinics and abortion doctors alike—is already embedded in the GOP platform, and I can introduce Kinsley to plenty of pro-life groups that spend a lot of energy on whole-loaf campaigns, from the sponsors of Colorado's "person-hood" amendment to the "Pill Kills" folks at the American Life League. But most pro-life successes, as I've noted before, involve incrementalism and compromise. If you're a pro-life group working on a partial-birth abortion ban, does it *really* make sense to kick off your campaign with an extended re-statement of their opposition to abortion at every stage of pregnancy? If you're trying to pass a parental-consent law, do you *really* want to start out by proposing that abortion be banned outright for teenagers, and only work your way around gradually to the provision you actually hope might pass? Most Americans already know that the pro-life movement has a maximalist view of what abortion law should be, I think, which means that restating your maximalism at every oppor-tunity isn't a savvy approach to negotiation—it's a good way to get people to tune you out.

Opportunies Push Issues to the Fore

What's more, politics is all about doing your best with the op-portunities that present themselves. Kinsley's right that once you get beyond the funding question, there's no necessary rea-son for pro-lifers to focus more energy on embryo-destroying research than on the general embryo destruction that goes on in fertility clinics. (Though research on embryos created ex-pressly for that purpose is another matter.) But the debate centered around research, rather than fertility clinics, during the Bush years in large part because the government's policy toward funding such research was on the table for review in 2001, creating an opportunity to nudge policy in a slightly more pro-life direction. No such opportunity, so far as I can tell, presented itself where fertility clinics were concerned—or at least, it hadn't until the public outrage surrounding the "Octomom" prompted some pro-lifers to see an opportunity to enact restriction on fertility clinics.

Which was, of course, the point of mentioning [in my previous article] "some law in Italy" (as Kinsley puts it). The law in question, passed a while back amid Octomom-style outrage over Italy's freewheeling fertility clinics, is exactly the sort of restriction that Kinsley claims American pro-lifers don't *really* support, fearful hypocrites that they are. Maybe he's right: Maybe Italian pro-lifers are just more serious and consistent than their American counterparts. (Catholics do tend to be more rigorous in their opposition to killing em-bryos than, say, Mormons—hence Orrin Hatch's support for stem-cell research, for instance.) But it seems more likely that the Italian pro-lifers are just making the most of a more fa-vorable political environment for clinic regulation than exists in the United States—and that if the American pro-life move-ment were suddenly transplanted to the Italian environment, its leaders wouldn't be shy about taking up the fertility-clinic issue.

We Mean What We Say

Kinsley concludes by suggesting that he's harping on fertility clinics for essentially tactical reasons: He thinks that the "fertility-anomaly hasn't even occurred to most pro-lifers," and "that when they realize that their logic in opposing stem-cell research would condemn all IVF as well, it will give many reasonable pro-lifers pause—maybe even about their pro-life position in general, certainly about their opposition to stem-cell research." Speaking for all the "unreasonable" pro-lifers out there, I don't think this is a crazy view of the overall po-litical dynamic. Just as lots of people who call themselves pro-choice blanch, for intuitive reasons, at abortions that take place after the first trimester, some Americans who oppose abortion don't really mind the destruction of embryos, and would look askance at a pro-life movement that sought to regulate fertility clinics. But there's a difference between this claim and Kinsley's initial one, which is that the people who are deeply involved in these debates don't understand their premises, and don't really mean what they say. I can assure him that we do. The attempt to apply one's principles pragmatically, and with an eye toward the art of the politically possible, isn't evidence that those principles don't exist.

| "Human therapy with embryonic stem
| cells matched to the patient is feasible."

Therapeutic Cloning Can Provide Patient-Specific Embryos for Stem Cells

Ann Carroll and Suzanne Kadereit

Ann Carroll is a former biomedical researcher and a policy analyst for health and science issues with the New York State Task Force on Life and the Law. She has been a faculty member at Albany Medical College and has authored many journal and research articles. Suzanne Kadereit is the science editor for the International Society for Stem Cell Research (ISSCR), an independent nonprofit organization formed in 2002 to foster the exchange of information on stem cell research. The following viewpoint is an ISSCR fact sheet prepared by Carroll and Kadereit that provides information on the promise of somatic cell nuclear transfer (SCNT), or what has become known as therapeutic cloning. The authors explain that in SCNT, the nucleus of a donated egg cell is removed and replaced with the nucleus from a skin cell, or some other kind of cell, from a patient. Then, through chemical or electrical stimulation, the egg cell is stimulated to grow and divide until it reaches the blastocyst stage, around three to five days later. At this time the blastocyst contains stem cells that potentially can be extracted and used to treat diseases or disorders in the patient. According to the ISSCR, SCNT provides a way to obtain stem cells genetically matched to a patient and so are not rejected by the patient's immune system.

As you read, consider the following questions:

1. According to Carroll and Kadereit, when and where were the first authentic primate stem cell lines created from a blastocyst after nuclear transfer in a monkey?

2. According to the authors, what are needed in large numbers in order for SCNT to realize future clinical applications?

3. According to Carroll and Kadereit, researchers at the Massachusetts Institute of Technology have combined nuclear transfer with what?

Human embryonic stem cells pose great promise both for basic research and eventual use in the clinic.

Embryonic stem cells are obtained from blastocysts, which are very early stage embryos containing about 100 cells. One potential problem for using these human embryonic stem cells for cell therapy is that the transplanted cells, which are genetically different from the patient, would be recognized as "foreign" and destroyed by the patient's immune system.

A Way Around the Immune System

A possible way around this problem would be to obtain human embryonic stem cells by a technique known as nuclear transfer, formerly called *therapeutic cloning*.

Instead of creating a blastocyst by fertilizing an egg with a sperm cell, as is done in the IVF (*in vitro* fertilization) procedure, nuclear transfer starts with an egg from which the nucleus (the cell's DNA) has been removed and replaced with the DNA from a body cell from the patient.

The use of the adult cell DNA ensures that all embryonic stem cells derived from the resulting blastocyst will be a match to the patient.

For several years now, researchers have successfully used nuclear transfer techniques to establish embryonic stem cell lines in a range of animal species, but not, until recently, from the primate.

In December, 2007, scientists from the Oregon Primate Research Center, Oregon, USA, reported the derivation of two stem cell lines from blastocysts after nuclear transfer in the monkey. An earlier report in March 2004 by Woo Suk Hwang and colleagues that they had successfully established the first human embryonic stem cell line after nuclear transfer of adult human DNA into a human egg was unfortunately found to be fraudulent.

The establishment of the first primate nuclear transfer embryonic stem cell line provided optimism that the technique will be feasible in humans and may ultimately be used for future clinical therapeutic cell replacement treatment free from immune rejection. However, significant hurdles remain. Most importantly, the procedure needs to be repeated in humans and the process optimized.

Remaining Questions and Hurdles

Need to refine and improve efficiency of nuclear transfer protocols.

Studies in different animal species have shown lower success rates for the derivation of embryonic stem cells from blastocysts created by nuclear transfer versus those blastocysts generated through normal fertilization. The reasons for this are not clear and need to be investigated.

To address this issue, researchers have begun to analyze the nuclear transfer procedures used in animal studies. In studies in non-human primates, for example, researchers noted that the method used for extracting the egg's DNA also resulted in removal of other egg cell components that are important for normal embryonic development. There also is evidence from some animal nuclear transfer studies that the newly inserted adult DNA does not behave properly. For nuclear transfer to work, unique components in the egg cell must allow for nuclear reprogramming of the newly inserted adult cell nucleus to occur. This ensures that it behaves as an embryonic cell nucleus would, and expresses, or activates, the required genes for smooth embryonic development.

Where will the human eggs needed for nuclear transfer come from?

For realization of future clinical application, it will be essential to address the question of how to procure the large numbers of human eggs that will be required. With current efficiencies and methodology, several hundred eggs, and many human egg donors, would be needed for a single patient therapy. Also, human egg donation is not a simple or risk-free process for donors. Thus there is a real logistical and ethical dilemma about how to obtain adequate egg supplies for large-scale therapeutic applications. Therefore, some researchers are pursuing new avenues of research and are investigating potential alternative egg sources.

Generation of egg cells from human embryonic stem cell cultures.

Some researchers have described the generation of egg cells from laboratory cultures of mouse embryonic stem cells. The researchers are now studying whether these egg cells can be used in nuclear transfer experiments. If so, this may also be achieved in humans and could provide an important new source of human eggs.

SCNT Embryos Unlikely to Develop into Humans

In the case of embryos produced by cloning or SCNT [somatic cell nuclear transfer], some scientists believe these human embryos would have little if any potential or probability of developing to the point that they could be born alive, certainly born alive and healthy. That is consistent with experience attempting to clone some animals whose developmental complexity and demands are much less than those of humans. If these scientists are correct, then it would be a mistake to ascribe to cloned human embryos even any significant potential to become a born human person, whatever the moral significance of such potential might be if they had it. And if cloned human embryos lack any significant potential to develop and be born alive, then the putative slippery slope from research to reproductive cloning feared by many opponents of the latter is not slippery at all; the former cannot lead to the latter.

Dan Brock, Journal of Law, Medicine & Ethics, *Summer 2010.*

Egg cell progenitors in adult ovary.
One research team found surprising evidence that adult mouse ovaries may contain a type of stem cell capable of forming new eggs throughout adulthood. If such cells could be found in humans, isolated and expanded in culture, this could open the door to a vast source of human egg cells.

Animal Disease Models

In addition to the hurdles remaining for improvement of nuclear transfer procedures, there are other aspects of the technique to consider. In order to ... use ... embryonic stem cells for therapies, it is necessary to induce the cells to develop into stable cells that function normally and show the characteristics and properties of normal tissue cells. At this point, it is not clear if the mature cells derived from nuclear transfer embryonic stem cells are the same as mature cells derived from embryonic stem cells isolated from normal blastocysts (that is, those developed from fertilized eggs).

Culture protocols by which the embryonic stem cells are pushed to become mature adult tissue type cells—such as functional blood cells, nerve cells, or insulin producing beta cells.

In one recent study, researchers reported that they could push mouse nuclear transfer embryonic stem cells to develop into the type of nerve cell that is lacking in patients with Parkinson's disease. They injected those nerve cells into a mouse model of Parkinson's disease, and saw some improvements in the afflicted mice. This result provided evidence that the specialized cells generated from nuclear transfer embryonic stem cells in the laboratory are functional when transplanted into unhealthy animals. Generation of other mature cell types from nuclear transfer embryonic stem cells, for example, insulin-secreting cells for cellular therapy for Type 1 diabetes, is proving more challenging.

Combining embryonic stem cell therapeutic approaches with gene therapy.

Researchers have begun to explore possibilities of combining nuclear transfer with gene therapy. These combined techniques would repair a diseased gene by introducing a normal gene into the embryonic stem cells, and would produce therapeutic cells for a specific patient with a genetic disease. A team at MIT [Massachusetts Institute of Technology] combined nuclear transfer with gene therapy in a "proof of principle" experiment. They used nuclear transfer embryonic stem cells in which a specific gene was repaired to treat mice with a genetic deficiency. The team first derived the nuclear transfer embryonic stem cells from the mice with the genetic blood deficiency. They then used gene therapy to correct the mutation in those cells. Then they grew the "repaired" nuclear transfer embryonic stem cells and pushed them to develop into specific blood cells, which were transplanted into the afflicted mice. The mice were partially cured. This study emphasized the potential promise but also the complexities of such an approach and identified additional hurdles that need to be addressed before applying it to humans.

While much progress has been made in a short period of time (human embryonic stem cells were only isolated in 1998), numerous hurdles exist that must be addressed before heading into clinical applications for humans. Importantly, ongoing research has provided "proof of principle" that human therapy with embryonic stem cells matched to the patient is feasible.

| "All therapeutic cloning must be con-
| demned."

Creating Embryos for Research Is Wrong

Christian Life Resources

Christian Life Resources (CLR) is a Wisconsin-based organiza-
tion that seeks to educate people about the biblical value and
sanctity of human life. In the following viewpoint, CLR says that
all cloning is wrong because it is not mankind's right to create
life. However, somatic cell nuclear transfer, or therapeutic clon-
ing, in which embryos are created and then destroyed, is worse
than reproductive cloning, because in the latter the intent is not
to destroy life, but to create it. According to CLR, therapeutic
cloning should be condemned.

As you read, consider the following questions:

1. According to Christian Life Resources, therapeutic cloning is also known as what?

2. According to the author, what are some of the ways that
   the term "soul" is defined?

3. According to Christian Life Resources, what are some of
   the disorders that cloned animals tend to have?

Cloning moved from the arena of movie-scripting to reality in 1997. It was in that year that *Nature* journal announced Scottish scientists had cloned a sheep named Dolly. The worldwide scientific, religious, political, ethical and moral implications of cloning continue to spread since then.

Human cloning produces the genetic duplication of another human. The genetic code is copied deliberately from one person to make another person with the same genetic material. A cloned embryo is a twin of its donor—essentially at an earlier stage of life. It is human and has only one parent with the same genetic makeup as that parent.

Three Types of Cloning

1) *Recombinant DNA Cloning* (AKA [also known as] "recombinant DNA technology"; "DNA cloning"; "molecular cloning"; "gene cloning")

This type involves the transfer of a DNA fragment from one organism to a self-replicating genetic element. The DNA of interest can then be propagated in a foreign host cell. This type of cloning creates fewer ethical concerns since it involves the cloning of DNA rather than the cloning of a human being.

2) *Reproductive Cloning* (AKA "somatic cell nuclear transfer" [SCNT])

This technology generates an animal with the same nuclear DNA as another living or previously existing animal. SCNT bypasses sexual [re]production by creating embryos without fertilization. The nucleus of a cell which contains genetic materials is taken and implanted into a hollowed-out egg deprived of a nucleus. The reconstructed egg is treated with chemicals or electric current to stimulate cell division. The cloned embryo is then transferred into a female's womb (or an artificial womb) until the clone is born. This process is already being tested on human subjects as well as animals.

A high rate of death, deformity, and disability is associated with this form of cloning. Dolly was cloned after 276 attempts.

3) *Therapeutic Cloning* (AKA "embryo cloning"; "clone and kill")

This type involves the production of human embryos solely for research use. To date, cloned embryos are used and destroyed within 14 days of existence.

Scientists harvest embryonic stem cells which can generate into any type of specialized cell in the human body. These stem cells are extracted from the embryo after five days' division. The extraction destroys (kills) the young embryo's life, raising grave ethical concerns from life-affirming organizations such as Christian Life Resources.

In November 2001, ACT (Advanced Cell Technologies), a Massachusetts biotech company, announced the first cloning of human embryos for therapeutic research. This breakthrough had limited success: 3 of 8 eggs actually divided and only one divided into 6 cells before the cloning ended.

The Issue Is Intent

Since all human cloning is reproductive (it duplicates [the] genetic code of the donor to make a new human life), the issue is really the *intention* for that life. The intent of reproductive cloning is to bring about a live birth; the intent of therapeutic cloning is to harvest the stem cells of the 5–7 day-old embryo and use those stem cells for therapeutic purposes.

Only God Should Create Life

God, in His Word, provides clear principles dealing with human life:

God alone has authority over life and death.

See now that I myself am He! There is no god besides me. I put to death and I bring to life. (*Deuteronomy 32:39*)

The LORD brings death and makes alive. *(1 Samuel 2:6)*

Man has the responsibility to preserve and protect human life.

And for your lifeblood I will surely demand an accounting. I will demand an accounting from every animal. And from each man, too, I will demand an accounting for the life of his fellow man. Whoever sheds the blood of man, by man shall his blood be shed; for in the image of God has God made man. *(Genesis 9:5,6)*

The commandments, "Do not commit adultery," "Do not murder," "Do not steal," "Do not covet," and whatever other commandment there may be, are summed up in this one rule: "Love your neighbor as yourself." *(Romans 13:9)*

Speak up for those who cannot speak for themselves. *(Proverbs 31:8)*

Human life is present long before birth. In fact, human life and accountability for sin are evident at the earliest stages of life.

Surely I have been a sinner from birth, sinful from the time my mother conceived me. *(Psalm 51:5)*

Before I formed you in the womb I knew you, before you were born I set you apart. *(Jeremiah 1:5)*

These passages direct mankind to respect God's authority over life and death. We do not have the right to assume God's authority for ourselves, but rather have the responsibility to protect human life, even from its earliest stages.

Other Cloning Risks

There is always the concern that human life will become a commodity rather than appreciated as a blessing from God. When the true value of human life is diminished, it is possible

Indignity Suffered by the Born and the Unborn

Cloning advocates have brushed aside moral concerns about human life, and ignored the indignity of creating new lives just to destroy them. Even if human embryos are "lives" in a biological sense, we are told, they do not have the value of persons—and they must be sacrificed to help born patients who really matter. Ironically, born patients (and adult women, exploited for their eggs) have joined embryos in being victimized by this agenda. In any case, we should not be surprised when an ethic that dismisses "Thou shalt not kill" in the quest for cures applies the same calculus to "Thou shalt not bear false witness." If the embryo's "merely biological" life can be trampled to benefit more valuable lives, "merely factual" truth can be sacrificed for the higher truth of Progress.

Richard M. Doerflinger, New Atlantis, *Spring 2006.*

to rationalize and justify actions that are otherwise considered unethical and harmful. The reality is that some already determine that a "potential cure" has a greater value than an existing human life. The risk is that this immoral attitude will spread as the value of human life continues to diminish.

The intent of therapeutic cloning is to destroy human lives within the first week of life. In spite of claims that this will benefit mankind, there is no justification in God's Word for such action. Therefore, all therapeutic cloning must be condemned.

Reproductive cloning is done in the same manner, but for a completely different intent. The goal of sustaining a human life is commendable and more desirable than the planned destruction of those lives, but the inherent risks involved in the cloning process make it hard to justify as a God-pleasing procedure. When considering the very low success rates and the subsequent destruction of the young lives that are considered "failures," this procedure as well cannot be supported or encouraged.

Clones Also Have Souls

The term "soul" is defined in many ways. For some it is an "inner strength" for others it is simply used as a figure of speech, but for Christians it is the part of a person, given by God, that lives eternally. It joins with the physical body at the beginning of life, and separates from the body at physical death.

Although God's Word does not specifically address the issue of clones, we do know that there is no life apart from the presence of a soul. If a human clone is alive, then we conclude that the living human being, regardless of how his/her life began, is a living being because there is a soul present. More importantly, we must conclude that a clone is equally in need of a Savior from sin and therefore will want to share the Gospel message of salvation with him/her.

> Do not be afraid of those who kill the body but cannot kill the soul. Rather, be afraid of the one who can destroy both soul and body in hell. *(Matthew 10:28)*

> As the body without the spirit is dead, so faith without deeds is dead. *(James 2:26)*

Cloned Animals

A tadpole was first cloned in 1952. Sheep, goats, carp, cows, mice, pigs, cats, rabbits, and gaur [a wild ox] have since been cloned by nuclear transfer technology. In 2003, a horse, white-tailed deer and mule were cloned. An Afghan hound dog, named Snuppy, was cloned in South Korea in 2005. The world's first extinct mammal, a subspecies of a mountain goat known as a Pyrenean ibex, was cloned using tissue samples from one found dead in early 2000; the kid, born in January 2009, died 9 minutes after birth due to malformed lungs. In April 2009 the first cloned camel was born in the United Arab Emirates.

Some species are more resistant to SCNT and cloning experiments have failed with monkeys and chickens.

Research involving cloning is very expensive and many institutions can receive lucrative funding for research. Cloning has had a high rate of failures, miscarriages and stillbirths. The rate of "success" of cloned offspring is less than 10 percent. For example, 841 horse embryos were created and only two dozen lived past their first week.

At this time, cloned animals tend to have immune dysfunction, aggressive behavior and increased rates of infection, tumor growth and other disorders. Studies of cloned mice show early death rates. Cloned calves also died prematurely and were disproportionately large in size. Australia's first cloned sheep died suddenly and mysteriously having appeared healthy.

Human Cloning in the United States

The U.S. House of Representatives has passed legislation twice to ban both therapeutic cloning—taking the life of a human at the embryonic stage in order to extract stem cell lines—and reproductive cloning for the purpose of creating babies with genomes identical to a living person. . . .

On March 9, 2009, President Barack Obama signed an executive order to lift restrictions on the federal funding of embryonic stem cell research. In comments made at the signing, Obama stated his administration would develop "strict guidelines" to avoid human cloning experimentation for human reproduction, because its misuse or abuse cannot be tolerated. Despite assurances by Obama that the government never "opens the door" for human cloning, critics say stem cell research can lead to the cloning process. . . .

The American Medical Association and the American Association for Advancement of Science issued a formal statement against human reproductive cloning. However, cloning for therapeutic reasons is gaining momentum in the scientific and medical world.

Periodical and Internet Sources Bibliography

The following articles have been selected to supplement the diverse views presented in this chapter.

CBSNews.com	"Adult Stem Cell Research Leaving Embryos Behind," August 2, 2010.
Ruth Deech	"30 Years: From IVF to Stem Cells," *Nature*, July 17, 2008.
Alla Katsnelson	"NIH, Stem Cells: IVF OK, Not SCNT," *Scientist*, April 17, 2009.
Jacqueline Pfeffer Merrill	"Embryos in Limbo," *New Atlantis*, Spring 2009.
Anika Mitzkat, Erica Haimes, and Christoph Rehmann-Sutter	"How Reproductive and Regenerative Medicine Meet in a Chinese Fertility Clinic," *Journal of Medical Ethics*, December 2010.
New York Times	"The Rules on Stem Cells," March 16, 2009.
William Saletan	"Drill Babies, Drill: If Harvesting Embryos Is OK, How About Fetuses?," *Slate*, March 13, 2009.
Science Daily	"Therapeutic Cloning Treats Parkinson's Disease in Mice," March 24, 2008.
Washington Times	"Embryo Adoption Becoming the Rage," April 19, 2009.
Rick Weiss	"Stem Cells and IVF: The Wild West of Reproductive Technology," *Science Progress*, August 19, 2008.
R. Werner	"Stem Cells, Human Embryos, and Ethics: Interdisciplinary Perspectives," *Choice*, April 2009.

CHAPTER 4

What Role Should the Government Have in Stem Cell Research?

Chapter Preface

The US government is the primary financier of most of the basic research that occurs in the United States. Human embryonic stem cell research receives a significant portion of this funding. Not surprisingly, researchers studying human embryonic stem cells are very concerned about the long-standing national debate over whether the federal government should support their research. State-level policies also pose a concern for embryonic stem cell researchers. Many states have laws that make certain stem cell research activities illegal.

Some states have laws that restrict a researcher's ability to create new embryonic stem cell lines. The creation of a new stem cell line generally requires extracting stem cells from a three-to-seven-day-old human embryo. In Louisiana and South Dakota it is illegal to do this because these states have laws that ban research harmful to human embryos.

The state of Michigan also has a statute that bans research harmful to human embryos. In 2008, however, Michigan voters adopted a constitutional amendment that trumps the statute. This allows scientists in the state to create new embryonic stem cell lines. The constitutional amendment—called Proposal 2—specifies that only embryos donated from IVF clinics and that are less than 14 days old can be used. According to Michigan Citizens for Stem Cell Research and Cures, the organization that spearheaded the passage of the amendment, "The passage of Proposal 2 gave hope to millions of Michigan patients and their families. It also freed our state's world-renowned researchers to utilize their formidable talents and use stem cell research to solve biological mysteries that have stymied mankind."

Michigan researchers seemed to have been waiting for the chance to make new stem cell lines. Nearly two years after the passage of Proposal 2, researchers at the University of Michigan created the state's first embryonic stem cell line, joining researchers in just a handful of other states, including California, Connecticut, Massachusetts, and Wisconsin. In April 2011, the University of Michigan announced the creation of two more stem cell lines. The stem cell lines announced in April are unique in that they carry genes for the genetic disorders hemophilia B, which is responsible for insufficient blood clotting, and Charcot-Marie-Tooth disease, which causes muscle degeneration. These are the first embryonic stem cell lines to carry these diseases, and they should help scientists looking to cure them. Bernard Siegel, the executive director of the Genetics Policy Institute, an organization that supports embryonic stem cell research, noted the significance of Proposal 2 in the University of Michigan's stem cell advancements. In an April 4, 2011, article, Siegel told the *Detroit News*, "The passage of Proposal 2 wasn't just a political statement. This has been followed up with real, tangible research and real results that have the potential to impact human health. It portends very well for the future of stem cell research in Michigan."

Researchers in Michigan are generally thrilled to be able to create new embryonic stem cell lines; however, they, and researchers in many other states, still cannot create patient-specific stem cell lines. The creation of patient-specific stem cell lines generally entails the use of a procedure called "somatic cell nuclear transfer," or SCNT. In the SCNT procedure the nucleus of an unfertilized human egg is removed and replaced with the nucleus of a somatic, or body, cell such as a skin cell from an adult human being. Once the somatic cell nucleus is transferred into the egg cell and stimulated to divide and grow, the egg technically becomes an embryo and can provide stem cells that are genetically matched to the donor of the somatic cell. So far only a handful of research groups have created human embryos using the SCNT procedure and no one has been able to derive human embryonic stem cells from an SCNT-created embryo. South Korean scientist Woo Suk Hwang had claimed to have done this in 2004 and 2005, but his reseach was found to be fraudulent.

Many states have laws that ban human cloning. Depending on the wording of these laws they may prohibit the use of SCNT to create patient-specific stem cells. Because a SCNT-created embryo is a clone of the donor of the somatic cell, its creation is banned in states that have anti-cloning laws. In Michigan and other states, including Arkansas, Indiana, North Dakota, and South Dakota, scientists are prohibited from making cloned human embryos. Therefore, researchers in these states are generally not able to create patient-specific human embryonic stem cells.

Some states with anti-cloning laws have written a loophole into the law allowing the creation of cloned human embryos for research purposes. California, Massachusetts, and New Jersey ban cloning for reproductive purposes but allow it for research purposes. In these states researchers can use the SCNT procedure to create patient-specific human embryonic stem cell lines. Generally, these states impose million-dollar fines on anyone who attempts to use the SCNT procedure to create a baby for reproductive purposes. Few American researchers are performing SCNT with human embryos as it is technically, politically, and ethically challenging. Those that are doing such research are generally located in California.

Researchers' ability to create new human embryonic stem cell lines depends on the type of stem cell line they want to create and the state in which their laboratory is located. This illustrates the important role that government can play in stem cell research. The authors of the viewpoints in the following chapter provide their opinions on what the role of government should be in stem cell research.

| "Public funds should directly support the use of human embryos for research."

Federal Funds Should Be Used for Embryonic Stem Cell Research

Laura Bothwell

Laura Bothwell is a doctoral candidate in the history and ethics of public health and medicine in the Department of Sociomedical Sciences at Columbia University. In the following viewpoint, Bothwell argues that federal funds should be used to support embryonic stem cell (ESC) research. Bothwell's argument hinges on the moral status of in vitro fertilization (IVF) embryos. According to Bothwell, either granting IVF embryos full moral status, as ESC research opponents do, or designating them as something less in status, as ESC research proponents do, relies on subjective belief. Since there is no middle ground between the two beliefs, Bothwell maintains, the one supported by the majority of Americans should win out. Since the majority of American society supports ESC research and IVF, Bothwell claims, federal funds should be used for ESC research.

As you read, consider the following questions:

1. According to Bothwell, the Department of Health and Human Services General Counsel has interpreted the Dickey-Wicker amendment to permit the use of federal funds for embryonic stem cell research, so long as it is not used for what purpose?

2. According to the author, the lawsuit that Judge Royce Lamberth ruled on was initially filed in part on behalf of whom?

3. According to Bothwell, that we live in a society with pluralistic beliefs does not justify what?

Dena S. Davis's recent Bioethics Forum commentary addressed Federal District Judge Royce C. Lamberth's August 23 ruling which granted a preliminary injunction to halt all federally funded embryonic stem cell research. As Davis pointed out, the primary target of Judge Lamberth's opinion was the Department of Health and Human Services (DHHS) General Counsel's longstanding interpretation of the Dickey-Wicker Amendment.

The Dickey-Wicker Amendment is a rider that has been annually appended to appropriations bills and provides that no federal funds may be used to create embryos for research or conduct research that destroys human embryos. Since 1999, the DHHS General Counsel's interpretation of the amendment has permitted the allocation of federal funds for research on stem cells provided that federal money is not used to extract the stem cells from embryos. The interpretation also has prohibited government funding of research that directly creates or destroys embryos. (The Dickey-Wicker Amendment does not apply to state or privately funded work).

However, Judge Lamberth's interpretation of the amendment would prevent federally funded researchers from using any embryonic stem cells because, on his reasoning, even if the extraction of stem cells from embryos were carried out with state or private money, extraction is a crucial step in the process and therefore part of the federally funded research.

Considerably compelling legal and scientific arguments exist against Lamberth's interpretation of the amendment. As of now, a federal appeals court has temporarily stayed Lamberth's preliminary injunction as the three appeals judges consider the case.

Meanwhile, numerous individuals who oppose the destruction of pre-implantation embryos have cheered Lamberth's ruling. As Davis has noted, for ardently pro-life individuals, the entire enterprise of human embryonic stem cell research is morally objectionable. All plaintiffs in the current case publicly ascribe to this position and indeed, the suit was initially filed in part "on behalf of embryos" and parents who wish to "adopt" embryos.

The current case is rife with ideological tension and moral overtones that are implicit in the Dickey-Wicker Amendment, its subsequent interpretations, and the motives of the plaintiffs. While the decision makes no mention of ethics, it presents an opportunity to subject the ongoing debate about the ethics of human embryonic stem cell research to careful public scrutiny.

Like Davis, I submit that public funds should directly support the use of human embryos for research. Here I offer a moral defense of this position by focusing on an element of the case which sets into relief the broader ethical debate—the moral status of embryos that are unused in fertility treatments.

In-vitro fertilization replicates the natural process of conception by creating embryos in the hope that at least a few will prove suitable for implantation. In the process, some embryos fail to develop. Sometimes, embryos develop that are not immediately needed. Most fertility patients freeze these embryos for later use. There are hundreds of thousands of embryos in frozen storage in the U.S. Eventually patients may finish their families and still have some frozen embryos remaining (so called "spare" embryos). They then have to decide whether to discard the spare embryos or donate them to research, including stem cell research, or to other fertility patients.

Current NIH guidelines restrict the use of public funds to research on embryonic stem cells taken from spare embryos donated for such purposes by fertility patients. Opponents of embryonic stem cell research posit that spare embryos are people who deserve the same human rights and social protections afforded to babies who have been born. Some have argued that it would be morally appropriate to force couples to implant all created embryos; however, this would introduce particular pregnancy dangers associated with multiple gestations.

On the other hand, a moral argument in favor of human embryonic stem cell research maintains that the spare embryos exist because technology has enabled more couples to become parents, creating more human lives than we would otherwise have. It is a great gift to humanity that the embryos left over from the assisted reproduction cycles can be used for research that has the potential to alleviate human suffering. According to this position, endowing spare embryos with the status of human beings fabricates a difficult and unnecessary set of social and moral obligations.

An argument in support of embryonic stem cell research maintains that the potential to become an autonomous human is not equivalent to being an autonomous human. This argument incorporates the integral role of parental decisions in the creation of life. Parents create children through a series of life decisions and events, and while the biological material of potential human life is a necessary component in that process, it is not sufficient. Equally necessary to the creation of a new human life is the choice of the parents to pursue pregnancy and carry it to term. A human being can begin only when all of these factors align.

According to this position, the biological material that precedes this point is morally neutral. Spare embryos are not human beings deserving of human rights and social protections equivalent to those afforded members of society. Therefore, it is acceptable to destroy these embryos in order to advance potentially life-saving science.

These are abridged versions of the more detailed and nuanced arguments put forth by both opponents and proponents of human embryonic stem cell research, and much thoughtful work has been published on the topic. The objective of saving human lives tends to motivate both sides of the debate. However, the recent court case elucidates a core challenge that seems to have resulted in a perennial debate over research on human embryos: whether or not one assigns full human status to embryos, one is relying on subjective belief.

Despite great efforts, it seems that no third position has been able to bridge the chasm between the two beliefs regarding the human status of the embryo. That we live in a society with pluralistic belief systems does not, however, justify a standstill on human embryonic stem cell research. To suspend research on account of irreconcilable belief systems would concede victory to opponents of research.

Meanwhile, as Davis has noted, the bulk of society supports both embryonic stem cell research and IVF. While majority rule is certainly not always sufficient argument for pursuing a specific policy, at least in this case, if federally funded research proceeds, opponents may at least express their moral disapproval by opting out of participation in the research, donation of embryos, or utilization of the products of human embryonic stem cell research.

> "By offering taxpayer dollars for [em-
> bryonic stem cell] research regardless of
> when the embryo was destroyed, the
> Obama policy ... incentivizes new acts
> of embryo destruction."

Federal Funds Should Not Be Used for Research That Destroys Embryos

Adam Keiper and Yuval Levin

Adam Keiper is the editor of the New Atlantis *and Yuval Levin is the editor of* National Affairs. *Both men are fellows at the Ethics and Public Policy Center in Washington, D.C. In the following viewpoint, Keiper and Levin contend that Judge Royce Lamberth's ruling on August 23, 2010, declaring that embryonic stem cell (ESC) research is destructive to embryos and therefore should not receive federal funding is in line with the intent of the drafters of the Dickey-Wicker amendment, who held that medical research must proceed hand in hand with respect for life. Keiper and Levin argue that if ESC research that occurs years after the embryo was destroyed is found to be complicit in the embryo's earlier destruction, then no portion of ESC research should receive federal funds.*

As you read, consider the following questions:

1. As stated by the authors, the Dickey-Wicker amendment has been law since when and as a part of what?

2. According to Keiper and Levin, the George W. Bush administration presumed the legal validity of Bill Clinton's interpretation of the Dickey-Wicker amendment, while looking for a way to do what?

3. According to the authors, when Lamberth's decision is appealed, the Barack Obama administration will challenge the judge's assertion of what?

Monday's [August 23, 2010,] decision from the U.S. District Court for the District of Columbia halting all federal funding of embryonic stem-cell research is a surprising milestone in the decade-long debate over this morally fraught field—and another opportunity to make the case that medical research must proceed hand-in-hand with respect for life and human dignity.

Interpreting the Dickey-Wicker Amendment

First, a little background. Human embryonic stem cells, which many scientists hope will someday lead to new therapies for a range of diseases, can be obtained only through the destruction of human embryos. But the Dickey-Wicker Amendment, which has been passed into law consistently since 1996 as part of the annual budget legislation, forbids federal funding for

> (1) the creation of a human embryo or embryos for research purposes; or (2) research in which a human embryo or embryos are destroyed, discarded, or knowingly subjected to risk of injury or death.

In 1999, the general counsel of the [Bill] Clinton administration's Department of Health and Human Services argued that, consistent with the amendment, the government can fund research that uses stem cells derived from human embryos, so long as it does not fund the actual act of destroying those embryos. This way, the government technically does not fund research "in which" embryos are destroyed. President Clinton proposed to fund work that used lines of cells derived from the ongoing destruction of embryos, but to keep federal funds out of the specific process of destroying those embryos.

Whether or not it was a valid interpretation of the letter of the law, this proposal was certainly in violation of the spirit of the law. By essentially telling researchers, "if you destroy an embryo with your own money, then you will become eligible for federal funds," Clinton's proposed policy would have incentivized the destruction of human embryos.

That policy never actually took effect—his administration ended before any funds flowed. When President [George W.] Bush came to office, he decided that while it might be worthwhile to use some public funds to see where research on embryonic stem cells might go (and particularly to develop cells with the abilities of embryonic stem cells without destroying embryos), it was important not to use taxpayer dollars to encourage the destruction of developing human beings. Presuming the legal validity of the Clinton administration's interpretation of the Dickey-Wicker Amendment, the Bush administration looked for a way to help scientists see where the research might go while not creating incentives for further embryo destruction.

In August 2001, Bush announced a compromise policy: He would use federal dollars to fund research on lines of cells derived from embryos that had been destroyed before his announcement, but not on any lines created after the announcement. That way, the availability of federal dollars would not act as an encouragement to destroy embryos in the future. This, Bush believed, was in line with both the letter *and* the spirit of the Dickey-Wicker Amendment.

Almost immediately, the Left attacked that policy, claiming that it was deceitful (not so), that it caused American researchers to fall behind the rest of the world (demonstrably false), and that it was part of a larger Republican "war on science" (ludicrous). To be sure, pro-life critics could truthfully criticize the Bush administration for not going far enough to protect human embryos. And scientists could correctly criticize the Bush policy for slowing somewhat the pace of their research—moral restraints will have that effect. But imperfect though it was, the Bush policy was a reasonable compromise that promoted research without turning the destruction of human embryos into a national project.

Believing that stem-cell research would be a wedge issue in their favor, Democrats overhyped it in the 2004 campaign. Four years later, candidate Barack Obama cast himself as a guardian of science—and once inaugurated, he overturned the Bush policy on embryonic-stem-cell research. President Obama ordered the National Institutes of Health (NIH) to develop guidelines that would allow federal funding to flow to researchers working on stem-cell lines derived from the ongoing destruction (with the parents' permission) of "spare" embryos frozen in IVF clinics—essentially implementing the 1999 Clinton policy.

Judge Lamberth's Ruling

Monday's court decision involved the legality of the Obama policy and the NIH guidelines. Two scientists whose work involves non-embryonic stem cells asked the court to enjoin the use of federal funds for embryonic-stem-cell research on the grounds that it violates the Dickey-Wicker Amendment. Mirroring Clinton's argument, the Department of Health and Human Services responded that while the amendment prohibits "research in which a human embryo or embryos are destroyed," the Obama plan funds only the research that occurs after the point of destruction.

Judge Lamberth's Opinion

Simply because ESC [embryonic stem cell] research involves multiple steps does not mean that each step is a separate "piece of research" that may be federally funded, provided the step does not result in the destruction of an embryo. If one step or "piece of research" of an ESC research project results in the destruction of an embryo, the entire project is precluded from receiving federal funding by the Dickey-Wicker Amendment. Because ESC research requires the derivation of ESCs, ESC research is research in which an embryo is destroyed. Accordingly, the Court concludes that, by allowing federal funding of ESC research, the Guidelines are in violation of the Dickey-Wicker Amendment.

Royce C. Lamberth,
Opinion in Sherley v. Sebelius, *August 23, 2010.*

In his ruling Monday Judge Royce Lamberth of the U.S. District Court rejected the government's reasoning. Embryonic-stem-cell research "is clearly research in which an embryo is destroyed," since by definition it requires the destruction of human embryos. It makes no sense, the judge wrote, to claim that the destructive act and the experimentation on the resulting stem-cell lines are "separate and distinct 'pieces of research.'" The fact that embryonic-stem-cell research "involves multiple steps does not mean that each step is a separate 'piece of research' that may be federally funded, provided the step does not result in the destruction of an embryo." The judge issued a preliminary injunction halting all federal funding of embryonic-stem-cell research.

Judge Lamberth's interpretation of the Dickey-Wicker Amendment is certainly in line with the original intent of the authors of that amendment, and with the understanding of the members of Congress who originally voted for it in 1996, even if the Clinton administration's interpretation (which was then adopted by both the Bush and Obama administrations) is arguably reasonable in light of the meaning of the term "in which." When the decision is appealed, the Obama administration will no doubt challenge the judge's assertion of the unity of all stages of embryonic-stem-cell research. Is the judge right to conclude that any experimentation on embryonic stem cells is, in the eyes of the law, inseparable from a broader research project that implicates the destruction of an embryo? On the one hand, it is true that all research on embryonic stem cells was preceded by and is made possible by the destruction of an embryo; the two acts are morally entangled. It is certainly clear, moreover, that by offering taxpayer dollars for the research regardless of when the embryo was destroyed, the Obama policy (unlike the Bush policy) incentivizes new acts of embryo destruction.

But on the other hand, imagine a young scientist just beginning his career, experimenting on stem cells derived from embryos destroyed years earlier, on the other side of the country, when he was still in junior high. Is he morally culpable for the act of embryo destruction? Is he engaging in what the law would consider "research in which a human embryo or embryos are destroyed"? If so, then the last nine years of federal stem-cell-research funding policy—under Bush as well as Obama—has indeed been in violation of a law passed by Congress in each of those years.

A Very Good Question

Whichever way the matter is finally resolved in the courts, it is certainly a great improvement to be asking this question—does the research being funded involve the destruction of human embryos?—and presuming that if the answer is yes, then the research should not be funded, rather than debating whether the destruction of developing human lives is of any consequence, and whether it should be supported by taxpayer funds. Putting the question this way, and presuming the incalculable moral significance of human life, was certainly the intent of the Dickey-Wicker Amendment, and should be the aim of any decent society.

But of course, the Obama administration and other champions of embryo-destructive research do not actually share this aim, and have always used the Clinton administration's clever loophole as mere cover. They do in fact want to encourage the destruction of human embryos for research, and they know that the Obama policy (unlike the Bush policy) would do just that. Judge Lamberth has called their bluff.

If the political climate and schedule were different, we might expect Congress to step in—perhaps with Democrats trying, as they have many times before, to knock the Dickey-Wicker Amendment out of the budget, or with both chambers moving on proposed legislation to fund embryonic-stem-cell research. But given the congressional calendar and the looming election, it is hard to imagine that Congress is going to do either—or much of anything else—during the remainder of the year. For the time being, this issue is one for the courts to decide and so, thanks to the Dickey-Wicker Amendment, the question is not whether human life is worth protecting but whether the government is going to sufficient lengths to protect it. It is a very good question.

"Bush got it right . . . to insist, in the face of enormous popular and scientific opposition, . . . on requiring that scientific imperative be balanced by moral considerations."

George W. Bush's Stem Cell Policy Was Right

Charles Krauthammer

Charles Krauthammer is an American Pulitzer Prize–winning syndicated columnist, political commentator, and physician. His weekly column appears in the Washington Post. *In the following viewpoint, Krauthammer contends that the discovery of a new technique to create pluripotent stem cells from skin cells (known as induced pluripotent stem cells) shows that the national stem cell policy set by President George W. Bush in 2001 was the right policy. Bush's policy allowed federal funds to be used for research on embryonic stem cells already in existence. But, as Krauthammer explains, Bush's policy prohibited using taxpayer dollars for the creation of any new embryonic stem cells. According to Krauthammer, Bush hoped that his policy would encourage scientists to find a way around the ethical quandaries associated with em-*

bryonic stem cell research. Induced pluripotent stem cells bypass the use of embryos, Krauthammer notes, and that proves Bush's policy was right.

As you read, consider the following questions:

1. What groups compose what Krauthammer refers to as the unholy trinity?

2. In contrast to where George W. Bush drew the moral line regarding stem cell use, where would Krauthamer draw his moral line?

3. According to the author, "providence" saw to what?

"If human embryonic stem cell research does not make you at least a little bit uncomfortable, you have not thought about it enough."

—*James A. Thomson*

A decade ago, Thomson was the first to isolate human embryonic stem cells. Last week, he (and Japan's Shinya Yamanaka) announced one of the great scientific breakthroughs since the discovery of DNA: an embryo-free way to produce genetically matched stem cells.

Even a scientist who cares not a whit about the morality of embryo destruction will adopt this technique because it is so simple and powerful. The embryonic stem cell debate is over.

Vindication

Which allows a bit of reflection on the storm that has raged ever since the August 2001 announcement of President Bush's stem cell policy. The verdict is clear: Rarely has a president—so vilified for a moral stance—been so thoroughly vindicated.

Why? Precisely because he took a moral stance. Precisely because, to borrow Thomson's phrase, Bush was made "a little bit uncomfortable" by the implications of embryonic experimentation. Precisely because he therefore decided that some moral line had to be drawn.

In doing so, he invited unrelenting demagoguery by an unholy trinity of Democratic politicians, research scientists and patient advocates who insisted that anyone who would put any restriction on the destruction of human embryos could be acting only for reasons of cynical politics rooted in dogmatic religiosity—a "moral ayatollah," as Sen. Tom Harkin so scornfully put it.

Bush got it right. Not because he necessarily drew the line in the right place. I have long argued that a better line might have been drawn—between using doomed and discarded fertility-clinic embryos created originally for reproduction (permitted) and using embryos created solely to be disassembled for their parts, as in research cloning (prohibited). But what Bush got right was to insist, in the face of enormous popular and scientific opposition, on drawing a line at all, on requiring that scientific imperative be balanced by moral considerations.

A Balanced, Measured Policy

History will look at Bush's 2001 speech and be surprised how balanced and measured it was, how much respect it gave to the other side. Here was a presidential policy pronouncement that so finely and fairly drew out the case for both sides that until the final few minutes of his speech, you had no idea where the policy would end up.

Bush finally ended up doing nothing to hamper private research into embryonic stem cells and pledging federal monies to support the study of existing stem cell lines—but refusing federal monies for research on stem cell lines produced by *newly* destroyed embryos.

The president's policy recognized that this might cause problems. The existing lines might dry up, prove inadequate

Drawing a Moral Line

My position on these issues is shaped by deeply held beliefs. I'm a strong supporter of science and technology, and believe they have the potential for incredible good—to improve lives, to save life, to conquer disease. Research offers hope that millions of our loved ones may be cured of a disease and rid of their suffering. . . .

I also believe human life is a sacred gift from our Creator. I worry about a culture that devalues life, and believe as your President I have an important obligation to foster and encourage respect for life in America and throughout the world. And while we're all hopeful about the potential of this research, no one can be certain that the science will live up to the hope it has generated. . . .

As a result of private research, more than 60 genetically diverse stem cell lines already exist. They were created from embryos that have already been destroyed, and they have the ability to regenerate themselves indefinitely, creating ongoing opportunities for research. I have concluded that we should allow federal funds to be used for research on these existing stem cell lines, where the life and death decision has already been made. . . .

This allows us to explore the promise and potential of stem cell research without crossing a fundamental moral line, by providing taxpayer funding that would sanction or encourage further destruction of human embryos that have at least the potential for life.

George W. Bush,
"President Discusses Stem Cell Research,"
August 9, 2001.

or become corrupted. Bush therefore appointed a President's Council on Bioethics to oversee ongoing stem cell research and evaluate how his restrictions were affecting research and what means might be found to circumvent ethical obstacles.

More vilification. The mainstream media and the scientific establishment saw this as a smoke screen to cover his fundamentalist, obscurantist, anti-scientific—the list of adjectives was endless—tracks. "Some observers," wrote the *Post*'s Rick Weiss, "say the president's council is politically stacked."

I sat on the council for five years. It was one of the most ideologically balanced bioethics commissions in the history of this country. It consisted of scientists, ethicists, theologians, philosophers, physicians—and others (James Q. Wilson, Francis Fukuyama and me among them) of a secular bent not committed to one school or the other.

That balance of composition was reflected in the balance in the reports issued by the council—documents of sophistication and nuance that reflected the divisions both within the council and within the nation in a way that respectfully presented the views of all sides. One recommendation was to support research that might produce stem cells through "dedifferentiation" of adult cells, thus bypassing the creation of human embryos.

Providence

That Holy Grail has now been achieved. Largely because of the genius of Thomson and Yamanaka. And also because of the astonishing good fortune that nature requires only four injected genes to turn an ordinary adult skin cell into a magical stem cell that can become bone or brain or heart or liver.

But for one more reason as well. Because the moral disquiet that James Thomson always felt—and that George Bush forced the country to confront—helped lead him and others to find some ethically neutral way to produce stem cells. Providence then saw to it that the technique be so elegant and beautiful that scientific reasons alone will now incline even the most willful researchers to leave the human embryo alone.

> "[Bush] certainly has earned himself a footnote in the history of science for doing what he could to block medical progress for political and religious reasons."

George W. Bush Had the Wrong Stem Cell Policy

Jeffrey Hart

Jeffrey Hart is professor emeritus of English at Dartmouth College and an essayist and columnist. He contributed to the National Review for more than three decades and wrote speeches for Ronald Reagan and Richard Nixon. In the following viewpoint, Hart argues that George W. Bush's 2001 stem cell policy was a serious blunder that was bad for the United States. According to Hart, Bush's policy reflects the beliefs of his evangelical and Catholic supporters but is not the policy most Americans agree with. Hart contends that Bush damaged the scientific preeminence of the United States by discouraging young American scientists from studying embryonic stem cells and making it harder for the country to compete in the field of stem cell research.

Jeffrey Hart, "Bush's Deadly Blunder," *The Daily Beast*, November 26, 2008. Copyright © 2008. All rights reserved. Reproduced by permission.

As you read, consider the following questions:

1. In what year did California voters pass a resolution authorizing the state to spend $4 billion for embryonic stem cell research, according to the author?

2. What book does Hart say the *National Review* and other conservative publications failed to review?

3. According to Hart, Bush joins the Catholic Natural Law advocates in the Vatican who sought to do what?

As we glance back at the gravest blunders of the Bush administration, let us ponder this one: In August 2001, Bush issued an executive order blocking federal funding for embryonic stem cell research except for some lines that were still in existence. "It's wrong to destroy life in order to save life," he explained. That required one to agree that a group of cells the size of the period at the end of this sentence is as important as a desperately ill human being.

Research Continued Despite Policy

Bush may have severely limited what research America could engage in, but he couldn't build a cognitive wall around the United States. Scientific developments in other nations were written up in refereed journals and became universally available. And support for Bush's position was crumbling within the U.S. In 2004, voters in California passed a resolution authorizing the state to spend $4 billion to support embryonic stem cell research. This immediately became the subject of litigation, but Governor [Arnold] Schwarzenegger enabled California laboratories to proceed by lending them money from state funds. With California now funding the research, American scientists who had moved to Singapore returned to work in California.

Private universities, Harvard and others, also went forward with their own funds. In 2004, Harvard created a multi-million dollar Harvard Stem Cell Institute [HSCI], which will occupy prime real estate in the vast new Allston science campus. Since 2004, the HSCI has been a leading force in research, making dozens of new stem cell lines available for scientists nationwide. . . .

One concrete example of what these efforts have wrought: A major problem has existed for the therapeutic use of embryonic stem cells. To prevent rejection of the cells by the patient's immune system, they needed to be cloned. That is, a nucleus from the cell of the patient had to be substituted in a donor's egg for the original nucleus. But in September [2008, *Washington Post* reporter] Rob Stein reported that in a major breakthrough, Harvard scientists have found a new way to reprogram cells backwards, turning them into embryos. Instead of using a retrovirus (as Japanese scientists had done) that can cause cancer, they are using an adenovirus which is safe. This would avoid the long-standing cloning problem.

Pluripotent embryonic stem cells develop to eventually create an entire human being. They also possess the capability of repairing damaged organs, and treating such conditions as diabetes, Parkinson's, Alzheimer's, and spinal cord and other nerve injuries. Bush's own bio-ethics committee, and its chairman, Leon Kass, voted in favor of federal funding, though with minor qualifications.

Evangelical Underpinnings

No doubt Bush's executive order reflected evangelical and Catholic support for his position, as seen with the evangelical leader James Dobson and the exponent of Catholic Natural Law, Prof. Robert P. George of Princeton.

But the following conservative publications also vigorously supported Bush's position: *National Review, The Weekly Standard, The American Conservative, Commentary, The Claremont Review of Books,* and *First Things. National Review* editorialized, "A single embryo must not be destroyed no matter how noble the goal."

None of these conservative publications reviewed Cynthia Fox's important [2007] book, *Cell of Cells*. Fox, a science journalist, described the vigorous embryonic stem cell research that was then going forward in Israel, Singapore (which was making a huge investment), South Korea, Japan, and China, in cooperation with the EU [European Union]. Some scientists in Egypt tried to start up a program, but ran into problems from their government—not ethical, but because they were exchanging emails with Israeli scientists.

Meanwhile, large majorities of voters and their representatives in Congress support federal funding but could not muster the two-thirds vote needed to override the Bush veto. But the political landscape has been changing.

Barack Obama has long been a vocal proponent of embryonic stem cell research, voting in favor of it when he was in the Illinois legislature. He continued to support it as a U.S. Senator, where he joined 40 of his colleagues to support federal funding. As he said in his supportive speech:

This bill embodies the innovative thinking that we as a society demand and medical advancement requires. By expanding scientific access to embryonic stem cells which would be otherwise discarded, this bill will help our nation's scientists and researchers develop treatments and cures to help people who suffer illnesses and injuries for which there are currently none.

John McCain voted for federal funding in 2007, thundering about thousands of frozen embryos. But during his successful run in the 2008 primaries, McCain, for obvious reasons, muted his support for the research with conditions, saying in answer to a questionnaire from a group of scientists that "clear lines should be drawn that reflect a refusal to sacrifice moral value and ethical principles for scientific progress."

Damage Was Done

Obama is now president-elect. He has promised to issue an executive order that will cancel Bush's 2001 order blocking federal funding for embryonic stem cell research. But how much damage has Bush already caused in the inevitable march toward stem cell therapy? The United States has the best scientific infrastructure in the world, and he probably has inhibited scientific work somewhat by blocking federal funding. Bush may have discouraged some of the best graduate students from going into the stem cell research field. He certainly has earned himself a footnote in the history of science for doing what he could to block medical progress for political and religious reasons.

In that respect, he joins the Catholic Natural Law advocates in the Vatican who sought to ban smallpox vaccination on the grounds that it is unnatural to mix human blood with cow serum.

All of this deserves a fifth book added to the four of Alexander Pope's *Dunciad*. [Eighteenth-century English poet Alexander Pope's satire on the literary dullness of his day was first published in three books and later, in four books, as he added other people he deemed dullards or dunces.]

> *"Obama's decision to permit federal funding of embryonic stem cell research is . . . the correct policy for the United States to follow."*

Barack Obama Has the Right Stem Cell Policy

Arthur Caplan

Arthur Caplan is the director of the Center for Bioethics at the University of Pennsylvania. In the following viewpoint, he asserts that President Barack Obama's decision to allow federal funding for embryonic stem cell (ESC) research using spare in vitro fertilization (IVF) embryos is ethically and scientifically the right policy. According to Caplan, the vast majority of scientists—the people who know best in this debate—believe that ESC research should be generously funded by the federal government to facilitate the discovery of cures for diabetes, spinal cord injuries, and other afflictions. There are hundreds of thousands of embryos stored in the United States and around the world, contends Caplan. It is absolutely ethical, he argues, to use these embryos for stem cell research, as Obama's policy allows.

As you read, consider the following questions:

1. Why does Caplan say it is hardly fair and completely disingenuous for critics to wonder why embryonic stem cell research lags behind government-funded adult stem cell research?

2. What was the single claim that the author says George W. Bush's opposition to embryonic stem cell research was built upon?

3. To what question does Caplan say that critics of human embryonic stem cell research have never given a persuasive ethical answer?

President Obama is carrying out his campaign promise to permit federal funds to be used for embryonic stem cell research.

This reversal of former President George W. Bush's ban on such funding is good news for the science needed to find treatments for currently incurable conditions and for the ethics at stake in the issue.

Research involving embryonic stem cells is still in its infancy. It has had a very hard time moving forward because the Bush administration would not allow the National Institutes of Health and other federal agencies to pay for such research.

But now that Obama is overturning that scientifically unsound policy, there are those, from the Vatican to right-to-life groups in the United States, who are complaining that, on scientific grounds, he need not do so.

The critics contend that there are other routes to get the benefits of stem cell research that do not involve the use of human embryos. Some opponents of stem cell research even have the chutzpah to argue that treatments using adult stem cells—which occur naturally in some parts of the human body such as bone marrow and the lining of our intestinal tracts—have been more effective in curing diseases then embryonic stem cells.

It is true that more than 40 years of federal funding of adult stem cell research has produced certain effective treatments such as bone marrow transplants. But after eight years of zero-budget funding of embryonic stem cell research, it is hardly fair and completely disingenuous for critics to point to the practice and wonder why it lags four decades behind government-funded adult stem cell research.

Scientists and Doctors Support Agressive Research

The people who know best—scientists and doctors—are nearly unanimous in the belief that embryonic stem cell research ought to be generously funded and aggressively pursued.

No one, not even some of the outspoken religious leaders who suddenly seem to find themselves possessed by the spirit of biological expertise, knows what the best source of stem cells will be for treating diabetes, spinal cord injuries or cardiac damage from heart attacks. No actual scientist can say with any degree of certainty whether it will be embryonic, fetal, adult, cloned or induced stem cells—those made by modifying adult stem cells so that they act like embryos—that will prove most effective.

It will take a lot of money and at least five to 10 years to find out. Uncertainty simply is the state of stem cell science. Keep in mind that nearly all of those who prattle on about alternatives to or the lack of cures from embryonic stem cell research spend precious little time with scientists or reading the scientific literature. Their claims about stem cell research are based firmly upon their religious beliefs.

So if I'm right and embryonic stem cell research is worth supporting with your tax dollars on scientific grounds then is it also worth supporting on ethical grounds? Absolutely.

President Bush's opposition to embryonic stem cell research was built on a single claim—that destroying human embryos is always wrong. But, even the president did not believe in his own moral principle.

Bush permitted taxpayer money to be spent on research using a few cell lines that had been made from human embryos before he became President. But, if it is wrong to destroy embryos to get stem cells then why would it be ethical to spend federal money to support such research simply because it began before an arbitrary date?

Even screwier was Bush's tolerance of private funding for embryonic stem cell research. If embryo destruction is blatantly wrong, then isn't it just as wrong if it is done by a private company?

Obama's decision to permit federal funding of embryonic stem cell research is—finally—the correct policy for the United States to follow. We have the scientific expertise and infrastructure to establish whether embryonic stem cell research can deliver cures. And we have sufficient moral consensus that it is the right thing to do. Obama's decision puts the sick and severely disabled at the center of federal research efforts— right where they should be.

IVF Clinics Warehouse, Destroy Embryos

The utter ethical incoherence of the policy that Obama is now happily putting to rest was reflected by Bush never doing anything to close American infertility clinics. Studies I conducted and that others have done show that human embryos are routinely destroyed at many IVF clinics for a variety of reasons as an unavoidable part of the effort to help the infertile to have children.

Not only do some clinics destroy embryos, others accumulate them—in huge numbers. When a doctor is not an immoral lunatic like the one who treated the recent mother of octuplets, Nadya Suleman [aka the Octomom], he or she puts aside some embryos so as to avoid the tragedy of mega-multiple births.

Research Should Go On

In recent years, when it comes to stem cell research, rather than furthering discovery, our government has forced what I believe is a false choice between sound science and moral values. In this case, I believe the two are not inconsistent. As a person of faith, I believe we are called to care for each other and work to ease human suffering. I believe we have been given the capacity and will to pursue this research—and the humanity and conscience to do so responsibly.

It is a difficult and delicate balance. Many thoughtful and decent people are conflicted about, or strongly oppose, this research. I understand their concerns, and we must respect their point of view.

But after much discussion, debate and reflection, the proper course has become clear. The majority of Americans—from across the political spectrum, and of all backgrounds and beliefs—have come to a consensus that we should pursue this research. That the potential it offers is great, and with proper guidelines and strict oversight, the perils can be avoided.

That is a conclusion with which I agree. That is why I am signing this Executive Order, and why I hope Congress will act on a bi-partisan basis to provide further support for this research.

Barack Obama, Executive Order and
Scientific Integrity Presidential Memorandum, March 9, 2009.

Over the past 30 years since Louise Brown—the first "test-tube" baby created through in-vitro fertilization—was born in England, more than 500,000 embryos have been frozen in American infertility clinics. There are hundreds of thousands more worldwide.

No one will ever use these embryos. They will never be put into a woman's womb. They will all ultimately be destroyed. Why would we not permit these embryos, which already exist and whose fate is sealed, to be used in research? The critics of human embryonic research have never given a persuasive ethical answer.

| "Mr. President, you make a piss poor argument in favor of embarking on what you yourself admit is an uncertain course of action."

Barack Obama Has the Wrong Stem Cell Policy

P.J. O'Rourke

P.J. O'Rourke is an American political satirist, author of several books, and regular contributor to the Atlantic Monthly, *the* American Spectator, *and the* Weekly Standard. *In the following viewpoint, he argues that President Obama's 2009 policy to allow federal funding of embryonic stem cell research is badly flawed. According to O'Rourke, Obama is mistaken to elevate science above morality. O'Rourke also asserts that Obama's belief that embryonic stem cell science needs government assistance is absurd. President Obama's stem cell policy is wrong and the argument he uses to support it is amateurish and poor, contends O'Rourke.*

As you read, consider the following questions:

1. What edition of the *Encyclopedia Britannica* does O'Rourke quote from?

2. According to the author, if the president wants to "kill little, bitty babies," he should do what?

3. According to O'Rourke, when listing the reasons for this research, President Obama undercut himself by introducing what new fear?

When a Democratic president goes from being wrong to being damn wrong is always an interesting moment: [John F. Kennedy's decision to invade Cuba's] Bay of Pigs, [Lyndon B. Johnson's antipoverty/antiracism program known as the] Great Society, Jimmy Carter waking up on the morning after his inauguration, [Hillary Clinton's health care plan] HillaryCare. Barack Obama condemned himself (and a number of human embryos to be determined at a later date) on March 9 [2009] when he signed an executive order reversing the [George W.] Bush administration's restrictions on federal funding of stem cell research.

President Obama went to hell not with the stroke of a pen, but with the cluck of a tongue. His executive order was an error. His statement at the executive order signing ceremony was a mortal error: "In recent years, when it comes to stem cell research, rather than furthering discovery, our government has forced what I believe is a false choice between sound science and moral values."

A false choice is no choice at all—Tweedledee/Tweedledum, Chevy Suburban/GMC Yukon XL, Joe Biden/Triumph the Insult Comic Dog. Is there really no difference "between sound science and moral values"? *Webster's Third New International Dictionary* states that science is, definition one, "possession of knowledge as distinguished from ignorance or misunderstanding."

What Science Has "Known"

Let's look at the various things science has "known" in the past 3,000 years.

Lightning is the sneeze of Thor.

The periodic table consists of Earth, Wind, and Fire and a recording of [the Beatles'] "Got to Get You into My Life."

The world is flat, with signs saying "Here Be Democrats" near the edges.

You can turn lead into gold without first selling your Citibank stock at a huge loss.

We're the center of the universe and the Sun revolves around us (and shines out of Uranus, Mr. President, if I may be allowed a moment of utter sophomoricism).

But, lest anyone think I'm not serious, let me quote with serious revulsion the following passages from the 11th edition of the *Encyclopedia Britannica* (1911)—that great compendium of all the knowledge science possessed, carefully distinguished from ignorance and misunderstanding, as of a hundred years ago:

[T]he negro would appear to stand on a lower evolutionary plane than the white man, and to be more closely related to the highest anthropoids.

Mentally the negro is inferior to the white.

[A]fter puberty sexual matters take the first place in the negro's life and thought.

The above are quoted—not out of context—from the article titled "Negro" written by Dr. Walter Francis Willcox, chief statistician of the U.S. Census Bureau and professor of social science and statistics at Cornell. I trust I've made my point.

What Morality Has Known

Now let's look at the things morality has known. The Ten Commandments are holding up pretty well. I suppose the "graven image" bit could be considered culturally insensitive. But the moralists got nine out of ten—a lot better than the scientists are doing. (And, to digress, the Obama administration should take an extra look at the tenth commandment,

"Thou shalt not covet," before going into nonkosher pork production with redistributive tax and spend policies.)

A false choice means there's no choosing. The president of the United States tells us that sound science and moral values are united, in bed together. As many a coed has been assured, "Let's just get naked under the covers, we don't have to make love." Or, as the president puts it, "Many thoughtful and decent people are conflicted about, or strongly oppose this research. And I understand their concerns, and I believe that we must respect their point of view."

Mr. President, sir, if this is your respect, I'd rather have your contempt or your waistline or something other than what you're giving me here. The more so because in the next sentence you say,

> But after much discussion, debate and reflection, the proper course has become clear. The majority of Americans—from across the political spectrum, and of all backgrounds and beliefs—have come to a consensus that we should pursue this research.

Mr. President, you're lying. There is no consensus. And you are not only wrong about the relationship between facts and morals, you are wrong about the facts of democracy. In America we have a process called voting—I seem to remember you were once very interested in it. We the citizens determine whether and how to spend the proceeds of taxation, which we alone are empowered to impose upon ourselves through our elected representatives in Congress, not the White House. If you want to kill little, bitty babies, get Congress to pass a law to kill little, bitty babies, if you can. I'm not going to bother arguing with you about whether it's wrong. Surely you too gazed at the sonogram screen and saw a thumb-sized daughter tumbling in the womb, having the time of her life. And a short life it will be, in a Petri dish. But we've already established that you don't know wrong from right.

Bad Politics

If Obama really wanted to resolve one front of the culture wars and show respect for pro-lifers, as he claimed, he would have refused to make citizens complicit in embryo killing by simply continuing the Bush policies. Instead, beholden to the radical fringe of his party, he chose to make a show of repudiating the Bush years. Not only was this needlessly harmful to our political culture, it may also have harmed Obama's political self-interest: he certainly didn't gain himself new supporters by wasting tax dollars on unethical and unnecessary research. In both of these ways, Obama's policy is bad politics.

Ryan T. Anderson,
Public Discourse: Ethics Law and the Common Good,
August 27, 2010.

Science Does Not Need Government Help

The question is not about federal funding for stem cell research, the question is are you a knave or a fool? I'm inclined to take the more charitable view. For one thing you have a foolish notion that science does not progress without the assistance of government.

Philosophy was once considered science. After Alexander the Great had accepted the surrender of Athens, he found Diogenes the Cynic living in a barrel.

"What can I do for you?" Alexander asked.

"Get out of my light," Diogenes said.

On the other hand, you, Mr. President, said that scientific progress "results from painstaking and costly research, from years of lonely trial and error, much of which never bears fruit, and from a government willing to support that work."

Thus it was that without King George's courtiers winding kite string for Ben Franklin and splitting firewood and flipping eye charts to advance his painstaking and costly research into electricity, stoves, and bifocals, Ben's years of lonely trial and error never would have borne fruit. To this day we would think the bright flash in a stormy summer sky is God having an allergy attack. We would heat our homes by burning piles of pithy sayings from Poor Richard's Almanac in the middle of the floor. And we would stare at our knitting through the bottoms of old Coke bottles.

We'd probably have telephones and light bulbs if President Rutherford B. Hayes (a Republican) had been willing to support the work of Alexander Graham Bell and Thomas Edison. As you say, Mr. President, "When government fails to make these investments, opportunities are missed." (Although the light bulbs would now have to be replaced by flickering, squiggly fluorescent devices anyway, to reverse global warming.)

Obama's Poor Argument

Also, Mr. President, you make a piss poor argument in favor of embarking on what you yourself admit is an uncertain course of action. You say, "At this moment, the full promise of stem cell research remains unknown, and it should not be overstated." And you find it necessary to say, "I can also promise you that we will never undertake this research lightly."

As your reasons for this research—which we are to perform with heavy hearts—you name a few misty hopes: "to regenerate a severed spinal cord," "lift someone from a wheelchair," "spare a child from a lifetime of needles." Then you undercut yourself by introducing a whole new fear. "And we will ensure that our government never opens the door to the use of cloning for human reproduction. It is dangerous, profoundly wrong, and has no place in our society." Because cloning cells to make a human life is so much worse than cloning cells from a human life that's already been destroyed.

Why, it's as dangerous, as profoundly wrong, and has as little place in our society as being pro-life.

Mr. President, any high school debate team could do better. Even debate teams from those terrible inner-city public high schools that your ideology demands that you champion no matter how little knowledge they provide. And I particularly enjoyed the part of your speech where you said that "we make decisions based on facts, not ideology."

| *"A major challenge posed by stem cell therapy is the need to ensure [stem cells'] efficacy and safety."*

The FDA Must Ensure Stem Cell Safety

Steven R. Bauer

Steven R. Bauer is a scientist at the US Food and Drug Administration (FDA). In the following viewpoint, Bauer maintains that it is incumbent upon the FDA to assure the safety and efficacy of stem cell treatments. According to Bauer, stem cell cultures developed in large quantities may be ineffective, or worse, cause tumors. Therefore, he explains, the FDA is developing guidelines and testing methods that will enable FDA scientists to evaluate stem cell treatments and assure the public that they are safe and effective.

As you read, consider the following questions:

1. According to Bauer, what does his research program use to study how cells multiply and differentiate?

2. What are mesenchymal stem cells, as described by the author?

Steven R. Bauer, "Assuring Safety and Efficacy of Stem-Cell Based Products," FDA.gov, September 16, 2010.

3. What are the major technological tools that Bauer says he uses to discover biomarkers on mesenchymal stem cells?

Cell-based therapies show great promise for repairing, replacing, restoring, or regenerating damaged cells, tissues and organs. Researchers are working to develop cell-based treatments that are both effective and safe.

Ensuring Stem Cell Safety

Many cell-based therapies use stem cells (SC) that are removed from the body and put into cultures in the laboratory, where they multiply before being infused into the patient. SCs are immature cells that replicate themselves and have the ability to give rise to a variety of different types of cells.

For cell therapies based on embryonic stem cells, stem cells are first stimulated to mature before they are given to a patient. However, embryonic stem cells can cause tumors, so products based on them carefully avoid having any remaining embryonic stem cells in the product given to patients. Also, these more mature cells may be better suited to replace specific types of damaged or lost cells or for repairing damaged tissue.

A major challenge posed by SC therapy is the need to ensure their efficacy and safety. Cells manufactured in large quantities outside their natural environment in the human body can become ineffective or dangerous and produce significant adverse effects, such as tumors, severe immune reactions, or growth of unwanted tissue. In response to this challenge, FDA [US Food and Drug Administration] scientists are developing laboratory techniques that will enable the agency to carefully evaluate and characterize these products in order to reliably predict whether they will be safe and effective. Our laboratories use cell cultures and animal models to develop such techniques and to study the biochemical signals that govern cell behavior during manufacturing and after administration to patients. These studies will help us develop testing methods that are practical and applicable to specific manufacturing steps. This will help CBER [Center for Biologics Evaluation and Research] to ensure the consistency, safety, and efficacy of stem cell–based products.

Developing Testing Protocols

Our research program uses animal models and cell cultures to study how cells multiply and differentiate (mature into specialized cells with limited, specific functions). We also study the effects on cells of their microenvironment, both inside and outside of the body. The microenvironment is the immediate area around cells. Parts of the microenvironment include other cell types, and other tissues and growth factors that have a localized effect on how the cells grow, divide, or migrate. Part of the microenvironment is the extracellular matrix made up of a carbohydrate-protein gel. The extracellular matrix helps to support the cell and cushion it from physical stress; it also serves as a means through which cells communicate with each other by releasing signaling molecules.

The communication among cells, as well as the time and conditions in which cells grow exert significant influence on stem or progenitor cell proliferation and differentiation. Progenitor cells are stem cells that have differentiated enough to be committed to becoming a certain general type of cell, and will eventually differentiate into a specific cell.

Our objective is to identify the molecules that exert critical influence on the growth and differentiation of SCs. Such molecules can be used in tests that evaluate and characterize cells during the manufacturing process and as lot-release measurements for cell-therapy products. Lot release tests are done before products are shipped out of manufacturing facilities in order to ensure their safety and quality.

A Spectrum of Safety Concerns

To determine whether it is reasonable to grant permission for a clinical trial to proceed, FDA evaluates potential risk based on results derived from analytical assessment of product characteristics as well as preclinical proof-of-concept and safety testing, which, collectively, are considered within the context of a proposed clinical study. . . . Due to the extent of their proliferative and differentiation potential, there is a spectrum of safety concerns that relate to a specific stem cell–based product.

Donald W. Fink Jr., Science, June 26, 2009.

We have developed tests that help us to determine how likely specific populations of progenitor cells called mesenchymal stem cells (MSCs) will successfully give rise to fat and bone.

One of our major efforts is the hunt for molecular biomarkers—molecules whose presence reflects specific states of activity, disease, response to drugs, potency, and other characteristics of cells and tissues. In order to discover biomarkers on MSCs we use a variety of technologies. Our major tools are microarrays (devices that enable the study of the state of activity of tens of thousands of genes at a time), RT-PCR (a technique for rapidly making thousands of copies of pieces of DNA), and flow cytometry (a technique for automatically identifying, counting and examining very large numbers of cells).

We are now studying the role of a protein called DLK in a strain of mouse that is genetically deficient in this protein. In these mice we found that DLK influences the generation of MSCs and their ability to turn into fat. Our studies have also shown that DLK influences development of B-lymphocytes, the immune system cells that produce antibodies.

We are also using MSCs from this mouse strain to study exactly how DLK helps to control the development of fat tissue and discovered previously unknown roles that DLK plays in this process. We've gained important new insights into interactions between MSC cells and between MSC cells and the cells that give rise to B lymphocytes. These studies will likely help us to develop improved methods for testing MSC products to ensure they will be safe and effective when used as therapies. This new knowledge will also help us to discover biomarkers for testing MSC-based products.

> *"It is inconceivable that a person's own cells could be classified as a drug—but that is exactly what the FDA wants to do."*

The FDA Should Not Regulate Stem Cells

Jeff Morris

Jeff Morris is editor of the e-Journal of Age Management Medicine *at Age Management Medicine Group. In the following viewpoint, Morris discusses the work and views of Christopher J. Centeno, an expert in the use of adult mesenchymal stem cells as a nonsurgical treatment alternative for orthopedic patients, about the US Food and Drug Administration's (FDA's) regulation of autologous stem cell therapies (i.e., adult stem cells extracted from a patient, cultured, and then reinjected into the patient). According to Morris and Centeno, these therapies could be revolutionary in the medical field, but the FDA, they contend, is threatening to regulate these therapies as "drugs," and thus taking the therapies away from individual doctors and handing them over to the pharmaceutical industry.*

As you read, consider the following questions:

1. According to Morris, what is the purpose of employing autologous stem cells?

2. According to the author, what are the three types of adult stem cells?

3. What does Centeno point to as the reason that it is important to be able to gather a person's own stem cells and bank them in advance?

Within the next 12 months it's possible that Age Management clinicians will have a new set of tools at their disposal—a whole new way of dealing with the diseases and disabilities of aging that is such a leap from today's medical options, it may well be considered Age Management 2.0. But it's also possible that those options may slip out of the grasp of physicians and become the exclusive purview of the pharmaceutical industry.

Christopher J. Centeno, M.D., is an expert in this area, having spent four years performing an autologous, minimal culture expansion technique in orthopedics that uses adult mesenchymal stem cells. Known as the Regenexx procedure, it uses a patient's own stem cells and blood growth factors to regenerate bone and cartilage. At Regenerative Sciences Inc. (where he also serves as lab director) and CentenoSchultz Clinic in Broomfield, CO (run with Co-Medical Director John R. Schultz, M.D.) the focus is on development of this non-surgical option for people suffering from various orthopedic disorders.

"The cell therapy industry right now is very nascent; it's where age management was 10 years ago," says Dr. Centeno. He has established an organization to set up guidelines and standards: The American Stem Cell Therapy Association (ASCTA). "We're trying to develop physician guidelines in the U.S. for the safe use of stem cells, similar to the way fertility clinics operate," says Dr. Centeno. "We've got an organization to formulate guidelines, and we've got clinicians working to form a stem cell registry. But the FDA doesn't like that. We only do adult cells from the same person, but the FDA contends that if you culture stem cells at all, regardless of the use of those cells, that's a drug." He points out that the age management community has seen many instances where the FDA has tried to insert itself into the practice of medicine—where it has been strictly prohibited by Congress from treading—and this is just the latest. "Compounding pharmacies have been coming under FDA pressure for a long time, and have now organized and set up their own standards and guidelines as a way to combat that."

Dr. Centeno compares the current state of stem cell medicine to the history of fertility treatments. "If you're a fertility specialist, you have to grow that person's cells at least to the blastocyst stage to use them, and the FDA has no control over that. If the FDA had gained control, you wouldn't have individual fertility practices—just a few big labs across the country." Instead of being regulated by the FDA, fertility doctors are regulated state by state. The reason, says Dr. Centeno, is simple: "They organized, put their own standards in place, and created a case, saying, 'Listen, this is the practice of medicine, and you're not allowed to regulate the practice of medicine.'"

Prior to becoming involved in stem cell research, Dr. Centeno was already an international expert and specialist in musculoskeletal, spinal, and neurologic injury. Having trained at the Baylor College of Medicine, Texas Medical Center, and the Institute for Rehabilitation Research, he is an M.D. who is double boarded in both Physical Medicine and Rehabilitation as well as Pain Medicine. Dr. Centano has seen the results that are achievable in an orthopedic context. "We've done this for four years for patients with orthopedic conditions, so as a test case, we know it can work safely and effectively."

To Dr. Centeno, it is inconceivable that a person's own cells could be classified as a drug—but that is exactly what the FDA wants to do. "The FDA is working to protect the interests of Big Pharma," he says. "If we wanted to insert some kind of new genes into these cells, we'd all agree that would be a drug—a new entity. But this is simply culturing a person's own cells. Most of the cells are bone marrow derived; you can get them from synovial fluid in the knee and other sources." There are three main types of adult stem cells:

- Mesenchymal stem cells are commonly found in the bone marrow. These cells can differentiate into multiple orthopedic, neural, organ, and other lineages.

- Very Small Embryonic Like Cells (VSEL) are a newer stem cell line with a more likely ability to differentiate into multiple cell types and lineages.

- CD34+ heme progenitors are usually derived from bone marrow and can be mobilized into the blood-stream. They have been used commonly in vascular and heart applications.

Most importantly, the mesenchymal cell line alone—the one Regenexx has been using—has more than 8,000 peer-reviewed references showing its wide application in age management medicine, including the treatment not just of orthopedic conditions, but of type II diabetes, stroke, and cardiovascular disease. "It can be used to treat everything from cardiac disease after a heart attack, to vascular disease, to orthopedic injuries," notes Dr. Centeno. As we move beyond "regenerative medicine 1.0"—which is where Dr. Centeno sees things currently—"I suspect what will happen in 2.0, is that you'll see some age management medicine doctors start their own regenerative stem cell lab, take cells from that patient, minimally culture them, and then they can be deployed." For instance, in cases of diabetes, the cultured cells would be injected under CT or ultrasound guidance directly into the pancreas—where, says Dr. Centeno, "in animal models they routinely get rid of diabetes."

It is important to note that while the recently lifted ban on embryonic stem cell research has helped to bring attention to the whole subject of stem cell–based therapies, the work that ASCTA does is related entirely to adult stem cells, and the patient's own stem cells at that. "A large number of diseases have already been looked at," notes Dr. Centeno, "the basic research is already in place." Some of the areas in which there is ongoing research on the use of adult stem cells in disease treatment, as presented in a "list-in-progress" on the ASCTA website, clearly overlap with areas of embryonic stem cell research:

- ALS-Lou Gehrig's Disease
- Alzheimer's Disease
- Multiple Sclerosis
- Muscular Dystrophy
- Osteoarthritis
- Rheumatoid Arthritis
- Spinal Cord Injury
- Stroke

In terms of treating age-related conditions, Dr. Centeno sees stem cell therapies as an entirely new generation of medicine. "In 1.0 we use hormones," he explains. "Treating using hormones is great, but at some point the parts wear out—and that's where 2.0 comes in." As an example, Dr. Centeno cites a study that was just presented at the American College of Cardiology conference in Orlando, FL, showing a dose response relationship on repairing the heart after acute myocardial infarction, with improved heart function after stem cell injection.

On March 31, 2009, *HealthDay News* reported on a U.S. study that found that "treating a heart attack with the patient's own bone-marrow stem cells boosts blood flow within the heart and may help reduce long-term complications."

The study included 31 patients who underwent angioplasty and stent placement after a heart attack. Within one week of the attacks, 16 of the patients received infusions of their own bone marrow cells into the coronary artery in which a blockage had caused the event.

The 16 patients received different amounts of bone marrow stem cells—5 million, 10 million and 15 million cells. The 15 patients in the control group received standard medication only. All the patients were followed for up to five years.

After three to six months, patients who received higher doses of bone marrow stem cells showed greater improvement in blood flow within the heart than patients who received lower doses and those in the control group, the researchers said.

"This is critical information for future study design—the more cells a patient receives, the more beneficial effect we see in the heart," principal investigator Dr. Arshed Quyyumi, a professor of medicine at Emory University School of Medicine, said in a news release.

The researchers also found that higher doses of bone marrow stem cells appeared to help cardiac function, as determined by measuring the percentage of blood pumped out with each heartbeat, and by measuring the amount of tissue death due to inadequate blood supply. However, these results were not considered statistically significant, the researchers stressed.

"These results show that treatment with a patient's own bone marrow stem cells has the potential to reduce long-term complications after a heart attack. We are encouraged by these results and are planning to conduct a more extensive study," Quyyumi said.

"Until now there was no way to treat that," observes Dr. Centeno. "Obviously, if you are a heart specialist or cardiologist this is of big interest to you."

The key to treatments using a patient's own stem cells is to gather and bank those cells in advance. "The number available to treat with goes down with age," Dr. Centeno points out. "In a 60-year-old person we might get 60,000; we can grow that in a lab to a million, which is enough to treat a condition. It's what the body does, but the body can't always get a sufficient number to the right place at the right time. If someone enters your practice at 40, just starting to see the consequences of aging, you would remove those cells and freeze them." Though this sounds relatively simple, the prospects for such treatments in the future rest squarely on developing industry standards in the near future. "There are already companies doing that stem cell freezing," Dr. Centeno notes. "The problem is if the FDA has its way, nobody will be able to use those cells because they will be considered a drug. You won't be able to use them in any meaningful way; you must incubate them to get them out of the cryogenic state because it's a delicate process"—and that's what the FDA considers turning the cells into a drug.

Thus, while development of stem cell standards and guidelines is a work in progress, it is one about which there is a real sense of urgency. "All of this could be done within the next 12 months; we could have hundreds of people across the country doing this work under the ASCTA," explains Dr. Centeno. "We could get out of the starting gate very quickly if everyone gets on board—but if not, the window's shut and it's never going to happen." The stakes for the pharmaceutical industry are obviously high. "You're talking about replacing $60 billion in drug and device care with $6 billion in stem cell care," Dr. Centeno observes. The end result will either be individual physicians owning and controlling labs, or, says Dr. Centeno, "It will all be controlled by Big Pharma, and innovation will move at a snail's pace."

Standards that must be derived include these, as enumerated in ASCTA's Mission Statement:

- To maximize patient outcomes by producing guidelines for the use of autologous adult stem cells (A-ASC) in medicine

- To provide standards for minimal culture expansion of A-ASC's and their re-implantation

- To establish that when A-ASCs are minimally culture expanded, are not biologic drugs but rather human tissue.

- To assert that the minimal culture expansion of A-ASCs is a medical procedure. . . .

Periodical and Internet Sources Bibliography

The following articles have been selected to supplement the diverse views presented in this chapter.

Ryan T. Anderson	"Obama's Illegal Stem-Cell Policy," *Public Discourse*, August 27, 2010.
Paul Basken	"Embryonic-Stem-Cell Research Wins Another Round Before Federal Appeals Court," *Chronicle of Higher Education*, April 29, 2011.
David Cyranoski	"FDA Challenges Stem-Cell Clinic," *Nature News*, August 17, 2010.
Donald W. Fink Jr.	"FDA Regulation of Stem Cell–Based Products," *Science*, June 26, 2009.
Meri Firpo and John Wagner	"Stem Cell Research in Minnesota," *Minnesota Medicine*, May 2011.
Kansas City (MO) Star	"Truce over Stem-Cell Research Benefits Missouri's Economy," May 8, 2011.
Lancet	"Embryonic Stem Cells, Francis Collins, and the NIH," July 2009.
Nature	"Stem-Cell Laws in China Fall Short," October 7, 2010.
New York Times	"Sense on the Stem Cell Front," May 2, 2011.
Wesley J. Smith	"Rule of Law Should Not Be Trashed in Name of Stem Cell Cures," *First Things*, May 8, 2011.
Rebecca Taylor	"Health Care Reform, IVF, and Stem Cell Research," *MaryMeetsDolly.com*, August 11, 2009.
Patricia J. Williams	"Science and Supposition," *Nation*, March 30, 2009.

Glossary

adult stem cells Multipotent stem cells derived from adult tissues, which generally only give rise to the different specialized cell types of the tissue from which they originated.

blastocyst A very early embryonic stage of development (about three to six days old) consisting of approximately 150–300 cells and composed of an outer layer and an inner cell mass.

differentiation The process whereby a stem cell becomes specialized into a specific cell type.

DNA Deoxyribonucleic acid, the genetic material found primarily in the nucleus of cells that contains the instructions for making an individual organism.

embryo In humans, the developing organism from the moment of conception (fertilization) through the eighth week of development.

embryonic stem cells Pluripotent stem cells derived from the inner cell mass of an embryo at the blastocyst stage that can generally give rise to any type of cell in the body except reproductive cells.

epigenetic Heritable changes in phenotype (appearance) or gene expression caused by mechanisms other than changes in the underlying DNA sequence.

fertilized egg cell An egg cell (oocyte) that has combined with a sperm cell and has a full complement of genetic material and thus is capable of developing into a human being; also called a zygote.

hematopoietic stem cells A type of adult stem cell that gives rise to all types of blood cell, such as red and white blood cells and platelets; also called blood stem cells.

in vitro Experiments that are performed in a test tube or petri dish.

in vitro fertilization (IVF) A procedure, commonly performed to help couples conceive, where an egg cell (oocyte) and a sperm cell are brought together in a petri dish in the laboratory, to produce a fertilized egg that can be implanted in a woman's uterus and give rise to pregnancy.

in vivo Experiments that are performed within an organism's body.

induced pluripotent stem cell A type of pluripotent stem cell artificially derived from a non-pluripotent cell, typically an adult somatic cell, by inducing a "forced" expression of specific genes.

multipotent stem cells Stem cells that can give rise to a number of different specialized cell types, but all within a particular tissue. For example, blood-forming (hematopoietic) stem cells are multipotent cells that can produce all cell types that are normal components of the blood.

pluripotent stem cells Stem cells that can generally specialize into any one of the over two hundred different types of cell found in the human body, except reproductive cells.

reproductive cloning Using the somatic cell nuclear transfer (SCNT) procedure for the purpose of creating a living human being that is a clone of the donor of the somatic cell used in the SCNT procedure.

somatic cell Any bodily cell such as from heart, skin, muscle, that typically has a full complement of DNA.

somatic cell nuclear transfer (SCNT) A process by which a nucleus from a somatic cell is transferred into an unfertilized egg (oocyte), from which the nucleus has been removed and the egg (which now has a full complement of DNA) is stimulated to begin development.

stem cell line Embryonic stem cells all of which are derived from a single embryo and are therefore genetically identical, which can be maintained and grown in petri dishes indefinitely.

therapeutic cloning Using the somatic cell nuclear transfer (SCNT) procedure to produce an embryo for the purpose of extracting its stem cells and using them to replace damaged tissues in a patient. The SCNT-created embryonic stem cells will be genetically identical to the donor of the somatic cell used in the SCNT procedure and thus will not be rejected by the patient's immune system.

umbilical cord stem cells Hematopoietic stem cells present in the blood of the umbilical cord, which are collected shortly after a child's birth. Umbilical cord stem cells are similar to stem cells that reside in bone marrow and can be used for the treatment of leukemia and other diseases of the blood.

zygote The earliest moment of human development; when the embryo consists of a single fertilized egg cell.

For Further Discussion

Chapter 1

1. Cody Unser talks about how embryonic stem cell research provides hope to people suffering from devastating diseases. Michael Fumento, however, thinks he should pin his hopes on adult stem cells or induced pluripotent stem cells. Which author do you think supports his or her viewpoint more effectively, and why? Which viewpoint is more powerful, and why? Overall, which viewpoint do you think is more persuasive, and why?

2. Michael Brooks says that patients should be suspect about international stem cell clinics advertising cures, while Aaron Saenz says patients are already hooked on stem cell promises and will accept any risk to get them. Compare the two viewpoints and identify where there is agreement between the authors and where there is disagreement. If you or your loved one had a condition that might be helped by stem cell treatments, would you take the risks of going to a clinic in a different country that advertised on the web? Why or why not? Use examples from the viewpoints to support your decision.

Chapter 2

1. Robert P. George and Patrick Lee contend that embryos have the same moral worth as children and adults because they are intrinsically the same. William Saletan finds many holes in this argument and believes that embryos are not morally equivalent to children or adults. Did either viewpoint change your mind about the moral worth of embryos? If so, how did your opinion change and why? If

not, using examples from the text, provide a short argument for what you believe is the moral worth of embryos.

2. Toby Ord asserts that those who claim that embryos have the same moral status as live humans must accept the notion that a scourge exists, because hundreds of millions of embryos are lost to spontaneous abortion each year. Do you think Toby Ord's reasoning is correct? That is, do you think if one believes in the moral equivalency of embryos to live humans, then one must be concerned about spontaneous abortion? Explain your answer.

3. Arthur L. Caplan and Pasquale Patrizio argue that a consensus is forming on the moral status of embryos and what can be done with them. After reading the other viewpoints in this chapter, do you agree or disagree with Caplan and Patrizio? Why or why not? Support your answer with examples from the text.

4. Andy Lewis says induced pluripotent stem (iPS) cells solve the moral dilemma over stem cell research, while Matthew Hoberg says iPS research has its own moral baggage. After reading both viewpoints, do you think iPS research is more moral, less moral, or morally equivalent when compared with embryonic stem cell research? Support your opinion with examples from the text.

Chapter 3

1. Maude Rowland, Kirstin Matthews, and Thomas Berg discuss the dilemma faced by couples who have surplus embryos after in vitro fertilization (IVF). However, Rowland and Matthews come to a different conclusion than Berg does on what these couples should do with their frozen embryos. Using Rowland, Matthews, and Berg as examples, discuss what factors cause different people to come to different moral opinions.

2. Michael Kinsley and Ross Douthat have different opinions about the "moral seriousness" of embryonic stem cell re-

search opponents. Kinsley says they are not morally serious because they do not oppose in vitro fertilization (IVF), while Douthat says that they can compromise on IVF without diluting their position on embryonic stem cell research. Which viewpoint is more persuasive, and why? Do you think that one must oppose IVF if one opposes embryonic stem cell research? Why or why not?

3. Ann Carroll and Suzanne Kadereit believe that someday it will be possible to create stem cells genetically matched to a patient using a procedure called somatic cell nuclear transfer (SCNT). Christian Life Resources contends that SCNT is not morally permissible because it is used to create an embryo solely for the purpose of destroying it. If you had to choose between using an IVF embryo for stem cell research or using an SCNT-created embryo, which would you choose and why?

Chapter 4

1. The Dickey-Wicker amendment is central to Laura Bothwell's argument that since a majority of Americans support embryonic stem cell research it should receive federal funding. The amendment is central, as well, for Adam Keiper and Yuval Levin's contention that if embryonic stem cell research destroys embryos, it should not receive federal funds. After reading both viewpoints, do you think the Dickey-Wicker amendment should be interpreted to allow embryonic stem cell research? Support your conclusion with citations from the text.

2. Charles Krauthammer applauds President George W. Bush for crafting a stem cell policy that drew a moral line between research that was acceptable and research that was not. Jeffrey Hart, however, criticizes Bush for representing evangelical Christians and Roman Catholics only and holding back the country's embryonic stem cell research

scientists. Which argument, Krauthammer's moral argument or Hart's scientific argument, do you think is more persuasive, and why?

3. Do you think P.J. O'Rourke's use of sarcasm and political humor in his argument that President Obama's stem cell policy is wrong is effective? Why or why not?

Organizations to Contact

The editors have compiled the following list of organizations concerned with the issues debated in this book. The descriptions are derived from materials provided by the organizations. All have publications or information available for interested readers. The list was compiled on the date of publication of the present volume; the information provided here may change. Be aware that many organizations take several weeks or longer to respond to inquiries, so allow as much time as possible.

The Center for Bioethics and Human Dignity
Trinity International University
2065 Half Day Road, Deerfield, IL   60015
(847) 317-8180 • fax: (847) 317-8101
e-mail: info@cbhd.org
website: www.cbhd.org

The Center for Bioethics and Human Dignity is a nonprofit organization established in 1994 in response to a perceived lack of Christian input in the area of bioethics. The center promotes the potential contribution of biblical values in bio-ethical issues such as stem cell research. The organization produces a wide range of live, recorded, and written resources examining bioethical issues, such as "A Review of Stem Cell Now: A Brief Introduction to the Coming Medical Revolution."

Coalition for the Advancement of Medical Research (CAMR)
750 Seventeenth Street NW, Suite 1100
Washington, DC   20006
(202) 725-0339
e-mail: camresearch@yahoo.com
website: www.camradvocacy.org

The Coalition for the Advancement of Medical Research was formed in 2001 to speak for patients, scientists, and physicians in the debate over stem cell research and the future of regenerative medicine. CAMR works to advance cutting-edge research and technologies in regenerative medicine, including embryonic stem cell research and somatic cell nuclear transfer (SCNT) in order to cure disease and alleviate suffering. The organization publishes various policy statements and FAQs about stem cell research and SCNT, including "Myth vs. Fact: SCNT" and "Alternative Methods of Producing Stem Cells: No Substitute for Embryonic Stem Cell Research."

Do No Harm: The Coalition of Americans for Research Ethics

1100 H Street NW, Suite 700, Washington, DC   20005
(202) 347-6840 • fax: (202) 347-6849
website: www.stemcellresearch.org

Do No Harm was founded by several scientists in July 1999 to oppose human embryonic stem cell research. The organization believes embryonic stem cell research is scientifically unnecessary, violates existing laws and policies, and is unethical. The organization acts as a clearinghouse for news and information on the dangers and failures of embryonic stem cells and the successes of alternative research. The organization publishes various fact sheets, background pieces, and reports related to stem cell research on its website, such as "Diabetes Treatments: Adult Cells vs. Embryonic Stem Cells" and "Recent Advances in Adult Stem Cell Research and Other Alternatives to Embryonic Stem Cell Research/Cloning."

Family Research Council Center for Human Life and Bioethics

801 G Street NW, Washington, DC   20001
(202) 393-2100 • fax: (202) 393-2134
website: www.frc.org

The Family Research Council (FRC) is a Christian conservative nonprofit think tank and lobbying organization formed in 1981 by James Dobson. Its function is to promote what it considers to be traditional biblical and family values and socially conservative views on many issues, including divorce, homosexuality, abortion, and stem cell research. The FRC established the Center for Human Life and Bioethics in 1993 with the mission of informing the public debate and influencing public policy to ensure the human person is respected in law, science, and society. The center publishes papers and other resources useful to the academic and political communities as well as to the general public, such as "Real-World Successes of Adult Stem Cell Research."

Federation of American Societies of Experimental Biology (FASEB)
9650 Rockville Pike, Bethesda, MD   20814
(301) 634-7000 • fax: (301) 634-7001
e-mail: info@faseb.org
website: www.faseb.org

The FASEB was established in 1912 by three member societies. It currently consists of over twenty societies, including the American Society for Biochemistry and Molecular Biology and the American Society of Human Genetics. The FASEB advances biological science through collaborative advocacy for research policies that promote scientific progress and education and lead to improvements in human health. The organization publishes the monthly peer-reviewed scientific research journal *FASEB Journal* and Breakthroughs in Bioscience, a series of illustrated essays that explain recent breakthroughs in biomedical research and how they are important to society.

The Genetics Policy Institute (GPI)
11924 Forest Hill Blvd., Suite 22, Wellington, FL   33414-6258
(888) 238-1423 • fax: (561) 791-3889
e-mail: bernard@genpol.org
website: www.genpol.org

The Genetics Policy Institute promotes and advocates for stem cell research and other cutting-edge medical research targeting disease cures. Each year, the institute sponsors a world stem cell summit, which brings together scientists and policy makers from around the world. The GPI publishes the presentations and views of those attending the summit in the annual *World Stem Cell Summit Report*. Additionally, the GPI issues a monthly electronic newsletter with up-to-date stem cell news.

The International Society for Stem Cell Research (ISSCR)

111 Deer Lake Road, Suite 100, Deerfield, IL   60015
(847) 509-1944 • fax: (847) 480-9282
e-mail: isscr@isscr.org
website: www.isscr.org

The ISSCR is an independent nonprofit organization formed in 2002 to foster the exchange and dissemination of information on stem cell research. The organization provides news and information relating to stem cells and promotes professional and public education in all areas of stem cell research. It publishes the *Pulse*, a newsletter that provides information on the organization, on stem cell research news, on scientific and industrial meetings, and on other items of interest to the stem cell researcher.

The Juvenile Diabetes Research Foundation International (JDRF)

26 Broadway, New York, NY   10004
(800) 533-CURE (2873) • fax: (212) 785-9595
e-mail: info@jdrf.org
website: www.jdrf.org

The Juvenile Diabetes Research Foundation is the leading charitable funder and advocate of type 1 (juvenile) diabetes research worldwide. The mission of JDRF is to find a cure for diabetes and its complications through the support of research, including embryonic stem cell research and somatic cell nuclear transfer. The JDRF works to effect changes in laws and policies that are favorable for diabetes research and to provide support for the parents of children with diabetes. The organization also seeks to raise the awareness of diabetes worldwide. JDRF publishes *Research Frontline*, an e-newsletter that provides the latest information about research on type 1 diabetes and its complications, and the magazine *Countdown*, which offers in-depth analysis about cutting-edge research and new treatments, as well as the personal stories of diabetes sufferers.

The Michael J. Fox Foundation for Parkinson's Research
Church Street Station, PO Box 780
New York, NY   10008-0780
(800) 708-7644
e-mail: info@michaeljfox.org
website: www.michaeljfox.org

The Michael J. Fox Foundation is dedicated to finding a cure for Parkinson's disease and helping those living with the disease. The organization raises funds to support human embryonic stem cell research and research into therapies that help those suffering from the disease. Actor Michael J. Fox, the organization's founder, frequently speaks out about the hope that human embryonic stem cell research provides to people suffering from Parkinson's and other diseases. The Michael J. Fox Foundation publishes a print newsletter, *Accelerating the Cure*, and an electronic newsletter, the *FoxFlash*, that provide up-to-date news about the foundation's activities and Parkinson's research.

National Institutes of Health Resource
for Stem Cell Research
9000 Rockville Pike, Bethesda, MD   20892
(301) 496-4000
e-mail: stemcell@mail.nih.gov
website: http://stemcells.nih.gov

The National Institutes of Health (NIH), a part of the US Department of Health and Human Services, is the primary federal agency for conducting and supporting medical research in the United States. The NIH is responsible for maintaining the NIH Human Embryonic Stem Cell Registry, which lists the derivations of stem cell lines eligible for federal funding. The NIH Stem Cell Research website provides various educational materials, FAQs, and scientific resources. The agency publishes comprehensive reports on stem cell research–related topics such as "Regenerative Medicine 2006."

National Right to Life Committee (NRLC)
512 Tenth Street NW, Washington, DC 20004
(202) 626-8800
e-mail: nrlc@nrlc.org
website: www.nrlc.org

The National Right to Life Committee was founded in Detroit in 1973 in response to the US Supreme Court decision legalizing abortion. The NRLC is the largest pro-life organization in the United States. The group has local chapters in all fifty states and works to effect pro-life policies by lobbying the government at all levels. The group also serves as a clearinghouse of information and publishes the *National Right to Life News* on a periodic basis.

WiCell Research Institute
PO Box 7365, Madison, WI 53707-7365
(888) 204-1782
e-mail: info@wicell.org
website: www.wicell.org

WiCell is a nonprofit research institute established in 1999 by the Wisconsin Alumni Research Foundation (WARF) to advance the science of stem cells. The organization focuses on enhancing and expanding the study of human embryonic stem cells by generating fundamental knowledge; establishing research protocols; providing cell lines, research tools, and training to scientists worldwide; and supporting other stem cell efforts. WiCell is tasked by WARF, the holder of human embryonic stem cell patents, to maintain the National Stem Cell Bank, which provides human embryonic stem cells to researchers throughout the world. The organization also provides training for scientists and offers educational outreach programs for K–12 students and the community. The WiCell website includes a FAQ section on stem cells.

Bibliography of Books

Michael Bellomo   *The Stem Cell Divide: The Facts, the Fiction, and the Fear Driving the Greatest Scientific, Political, and Religious Debate of Our Time.* New York: American Management Association, 2006.

Laura Black   *The Stem Cell Debate: The Ethics and Science Behind the Research.* Berkeley Heights, NJ: Enslow, 2006.

Thomas C.G. Bosch   *Stem Cells: From Hydra to Man.* New York: Springer, 2010.

John Bryant, Linda Baggott la Velle, and John Searle   *Introduction to Bioethics.* Hoboken, NJ: Wiley, 2005.

Eileen L. Daniel, ed.   *Taking Sides: Clashing Views in Health and Society.* Dubuque, IA: McGraw Hill, 2006.

Catherine Ennis, Emer Clarke, Christopher Lannon, and Eric Atkinson   *Introduction to Stem Cell Science.* Wellington, FL: Genetics Policy Institute, 2011.

Cynthia Fox   *Cell of Cells: The Global Race to Capture and Control the Stem Cell.* New York: Norton, 2006.

Lawrence Goldstein and Meg Schneider   *Stem Cells for Dummies.* Hoboken, NJ: Wiley, 2010.

Judith A. Johnson and Erin D. Williams — *CRS Report for Congress: Stem Cell Research*. Washington, DC: Government Printing Office, 2005.

Helga Kuhse and Peter Singer, eds. — *Bioethics: An Anthology*. Malden, MA: Blackwell, 2006.

Robert Lanza et al., eds. — *Essentials of Stem Cell Biology*. Burlington, MA: Elsevier Academic, 2005.

Jane Maienschein — *Whose View of Life? Embryos, Cloning, and Stem Cells*. Cambridge, MA: Harvard University Press, 2004.

Steven Paul McGiffen — *Biotechnology: Corporate Power Versus the Public Interest*. London: Pluto, 2005.

Chris Mooney — *The Republican War on Science*. New York: Basic Books, 2005.

Christine Mummery, Sir Ian Wilmut, Anja Van De Stolpe, and Bernard Roelen — *Stem Cells: Scientific Facts and Fiction*. Burlington, MA: Elsevier Academic, 2011.

National Research Council and Institute of Medicine — *Guidelines for Human Embryonic Stem Cell Research*. Washington, DC: National Academies Press, 2005.

Lars Ostner — *Stem Cells, Human Embryos, and Ethics: Interdisciplinary Perspectives*. New York: Springer, 2008.

Eve Herold Palgrave	*Stem Cell Wars: Inside Stories from the Frontlines.* New York: Macmillan, 2006.
Joseph Panno	*Stem Cell Research: Medical Applications and Ethical Controversy.* New York: Facts On File, 2005.
Ann B. Parson	*The Proteus Effect: Stem Cells and Their Promise for Medicine.* Washington, DC: Joseph Henry Press, 2004.
Ted Peters, Karen Lebacqz, and Gayman Bennett	*Sacred Cells? Why Christians Should Support Stem Cell Research.* Lanham, MD: Rowman & Littlefield, 2008.
Albert Sasson	*Medical Biotechnology: Achievements, Prospects, and Perceptions.* New York: United Nations University Press, 2005.
Christopher Thomas Scott	*Stem Cell Now: From the Experiment That Shook the World to the New Politics of Life.* New York: Pi Press, 2006.
Nancy E. Snow, ed.	*Stem Cell Research: New Frontiers in Science and Ethics.* Notre Dame, IN: University of Notre Dame Press, 2004.
Wendy Wagner and Rena Steinzor	*Rescuing Science from Politics: Regulation and the Distortion of Scientific Research.* New York: Cambridge University Press, 2006.

Ian Wilmut and Roger Highfield — *After Dolly: The Uses and Misuses of Human Cloning*. New York: Norton, 2006.

Index

I

J

K